SpringerBriefs in International Relations

SpringerBriefs present concise summaries of cutting-edge research and practical applications across a wide spectrum of fields. Featuring compact volumes of 50 to 125 pages, the series covers a range of content from professional to academic. Typical topics might include:

A timely report of state-of-the art analytical techniques

A bridge between new research results, as published in journal articles, and a contextual literature review

A snapshot of a hot or emerging topic

An in-depth case study or clinical example

A presentation of core concepts that students must understand in order to make independent contributions

SpringerBriefs in International Relations showcase emerging theory, empirical research, and practical application in all areas of international relations from a global author community. Topics include, but are not limited to, IR-theory, international security studies, foreign policy, peace and conflict studies, international organization, global governance, international political economy, the history of international relations and related fields.

SpringerBriefs are characterized by fast, global electronic dissemination, standard publishing contracts, standardized manuscript preparation and formatting guidelines, and expedited production schedules.

Julian Walterskirchen • Gerhard Mangott •
Clara Wend

Sanction Dynamics in the Cases of North Korea, Iran, and Russia

Objectives, Measures and Effects

Julian Walterskirchen
Center for Intelligence and
Security Studies
Bundeswehr University Munich
Neubiberg, Germany

Gerhard Mangott
Department of Political Science
Universität Innsbruck
Innsbruck, Austria

Clara Wend
Department of Political Science
Universität Innsbruck
Innsbruck, Austria

ISSN 2731-3352   ISSN 2731-3360   (electronic)
SpringerBriefs in International Relations
ISBN 978-3-031-17396-7   ISBN 978-3-031-17397-4   (eBook)
https://doi.org/10.1007/978-3-031-17397-4

© The Author(s), under exclusive license to Springer Nature Switzerland AG 2022

This work is subject to copyright. All rights are solely and exclusively licensed by the Publisher, whether the whole or part of the material is concerned, specifically the rights of translation, reprinting, reuse of illustrations, recitation, broadcasting, reproduction on microfilms or in any other physical way, and transmission or information storage and retrieval, electronic adaptation, computer software, or by similar or dissimilar methodology now known or hereafter developed.

The use of general descriptive names, registered names, trademarks, service marks, etc. in this publication does not imply, even in the absence of a specific statement, that such names are exempt from the relevant protective laws and regulations and therefore free for general use.

The publisher, the authors, and the editors are safe to assume that the advice and information in this book are believed to be true and accurate at the date of publication. Neither the publisher nor the authors or the editors give a warranty, expressed or implied, with respect to the material contained herein or for any errors or omissions that may have been made. The publisher remains neutral with regard to jurisdictional claims in published maps and institutional affiliations.

This Springer imprint is published by the registered company Springer Nature Switzerland AG
The registered company address is: Gewerbestrasse 11, 6330 Cham, Switzerland

Acknowledgement

This project was facilitated by the Anniversary Fund of the Austrian National Bank (Jubiläumsfonds der Oesterreichischen Nationalbank).

About the Book

The application of sanctions as a foreign policy tool has developed considerably, particularly over the last three decades. Many states and international organizations seem to have embraced sanctions as their go-to tool when dealing with international crisis. This report investigates the sanctions regimes imposed by the USA, the European Union, and the United Nations against Russia, Iran, and North Korea. It analyzes the dynamic nature of sanctions imposition and focuses on understanding the multi-layered objectives sender countries pursue, the type of measures they impose, as well as disentangling the effects sanctions have. Furthermore, this report analyzes the countermeasures the targeted countries take to decrease the impact of the sanctions on their economy, to circumvent them, or to impose costs on the sender countries. The main insights gained through the analysis of the sanctions against Russia, Iran, and North Korea are summarized below:

- Senders seek to achieve a wide array of goals, sometimes simultaneously, with their sanctions measures, and these goals not only differ between states that are part of the same sanctioning coalition, but they can also drastically change over time depending on shifting domestic political priorities.
- Sanctions regimes constantly need to evolve in the face of changes in the international system as well as developments in the targeted countries. Furthermore, while the UN Security Council can be one of the most important actors to create coherent sanctions regimes, it is at times not flexible enough to adjust to newer developments, due to the time-consuming but necessary consensus building between the permanent members of the Security Council. In contrast, the EU and the USA are becoming increasingly willing to impose sanctions measures in response to a broader set of security challenges.
- The effects of sanctions in the cases of Russia and North Korea can only be considered as relatively weak, either because they were initially not far reaching enough or because exposure to the global economy was already almost non-existent or limited. In the case of Iran, the effect of sanctions seems to be more substantial, as sanctions have contributed to Iran agreeing to the JCPOA in 2015. US sanctions also had a substantial negative impact on Iran's economy

after their reintroduction in 2018. However, while many of the sanctions were designed to be specifically targeted at entities and persons that are directly involved with the sanctioned behavior, there seems to be evidence that the elites in question were able to mostly avoid direct negative effects. In addition, while there is some evidence that sanctions have negatively affected the targeted economies, the sanctions so far have failed to achieve their political goals.

- Countries that are targets of sanctions seek to adopt countermeasures. Stronger countries can leverage a larger number of measures to deal with the negative consequences imposed by sanctions. Weaker countries focus their efforts on seeking illicit ways to avoid sanctions, such as illicit maritime activity and seeking to hide transactions behind opaque business and financial structures.
- Sanctions can have an immediate economic effect, however, it seems that for this economic effect to translate into a political effect the costs imposed have to be maintained and hence sanctions should be viewed as mid- to long-term tools. This also necessitates to view sanctions not as a strategy in its own right but as a tool that has to be carefully balanced with other available foreign policy tools.
- Sanctions measures are more effective if they are linked to specific and clearly articulated goals. Sender countries should put special emphasis on communicating its expectations of the target country as well as specific steps that could lead to a reduction or lifting of sanctions. In line with this, sender countries should seek to limit their goals to realistically achievable change in behavior, particularly when dealing with stronger countries.
- Sender countries need to understand the imposition of sanctions as a dynamic process between multiple actors. Given that targeted states will seek to minimize the costs imposed by sanctions, they will seek to adjust to circumvent sanctions. Hence, sanctions regimes need to be closely monitored and sender countries need to be flexible to successfully adjust the sanctions measures to reflect the new circumstances.
- Sanctions are more effective when based on a broad multilateral coalition. In the best case they are mandated by the United Nations Security Council and hence almost universal and mandatory.

Contents

1 Introduction 1
2 Objectives 3
   2.1 Iran 5
   2.2 North Korea 10
   2.3 Russia 12
3 Measures 15
   3.1 Trends in Sanctions Imposition 16
   3.2 Iran 17
   3.3 North Korea 20
   3.4 Russia 25
4 Effects of Sanctions on North Korea, Iran, and Russia ... 33
   4.1 Iran 34
   4.2 North Korea 36
   4.3 Russia 39
5 Countermeasures 47
   5.1 Iran 47
   5.2 North Korea 48
   5.3 Russia 52
6 Recent Developments 55
   6.1 Iran 55
   6.2 North Korea 57
   6.3 Russia 58
      6.3.1 Russia's Invasion of Ukraine 59
7 Conclusion 65

References 71

Chapter 1
Introduction

Sanctions have become an increasingly important foreign policy tool for policymakers over the past 30 years (see, e.g., Allen, 2005). Moreover, while sanctions have been part of the foreign policy toolkit of many states and international organizations throughout most of modern history, they have mostly been employed preceding or in addition to using military force (Kern, 2009). Only more recently have sanctions received attention as a stand-alone or primary means to achieving foreign policy objectives. Furthermore, the range of challenges sanctions are being used to address has increased, ranging from breaches of territorial sovereignty, human rights violations to issues of nuclear proliferation and the fight against transnational terrorism. Sanctions are also increasingly used to target a myriad of different actors, including terrorist organizations, politicians, banks, companies, and even criminal organizations like drug cartels. These trends are supported by recent findings by Morgan et al. (2014), who provided empirical records that suggest that sanctions utilization by policymakers has risen significantly in the 1990s and despite a slight decline in the 2000s has remained high ever since. These trends have also led to an increased interest and attention to the topic of sanctions in academic circles and consequently have led to an increase in scholarly work on this issue.

However, the academic debate has been more diverse and has retained, to a certain degree, a pervasively pessimistic view of sanction's utility to coerce another state to change its policies or behavior (Kirshner, 2002, p. 160). Yet, this has raised an ostensible question: Why would policymakers make use of an instrument, whose success remains more or less the exception rather than the rule? Some have argued that sanctions may not be primarily aimed at coercion, but may have other objectives, whose utilities to policymakers have been overlooked. Subsequently, some scholars have proposed what they perceived a more fruitful research direction

---

Supplementary Information The online version contains supplementary material available at https://doi.org/10.1007/978-3-031-17397-4_1.

(Blanchard & Ripsman, 1999, p. 220). They were less interested in whether sanctions do, indeed, work (or not) but rather when they are more likely to do so. Many factors have been examined and considered possible determinants of sanction effectiveness. More recent empirical findings have even suggested a more optimistic view (see, e.g., Hufbauer et al., 1990, 2007; Morgan et al., 2014; Felbermayr et al., 2020). However, empirical findings have often been inconclusive. Some have perceived the applied models and often diverging variables therein to be responsible, while still others refer to inherent biases in case selection (see, e.g., Bapat et al., 2013; Drezner, 2003). Furthermore, Drezner (2011, p. 96) has argued that the sanction literature suffers from an inherent sender bias and thus neglects how the target can respond to sanctions. Moreover, while theoretical arguments and typologies have long considered the possibility of multiple sender objectives, most studies have not comprehensively and coherently approached this issue. Consequentially and as Drury (2001) states, "[...] we do not have a comprehensive understanding of this important foreign policy."

Nonetheless, while our understanding of how sanctions work, when they are employed and how effective they are in achieving their respective objectives has greatly improved due to decades of invaluable research, there are still open questions researchers have failed to adequately address this far. Most notably, researchers have failed to disaggregate sanctions measures and objectives, as well as taking into account countermeasures targets of sanctions can employ to mitigate their effectiveness. Furthermore, the issue of the effect of sanctions that has so far not been answered conclusively (see, e.g., Bapat et al., 2013; Bapat & Kwon, 2015; Galtung, 1967; Hufbauer et al., 2007; Tsebelis, 1990; Vines, 2012). This report seeks to address some of these limitations in previous studies of sanctions by investigating individual sanctions measures, their objectives as a foreign policy tool, their effects on the targeted economies and governments, and how targeted states respond to them. After the introduction this report will proceed as follows: First, the objectives sender countries pursue when imposing sanctions measures will be investigated. This will be followed by a section that addresses in detail which sanctions measures sender countries have imposed in these three cases. The third section aims at identifying and distinguishing the political and economic effects sanctions have on the targeted countries and locate these in broader economic trends. In a next section, this report seeks to identify the countermeasures the targeted countries employ in order to diminish the negative effects sanctions could have on their economies. This will be followed by a brief overview of recent developments in the cases of Iran, North Korea, and Russia. Finally, the report will seek to give a concise summary of the most important aspects identified in the previous sections and some key characteristics will be described that could improve the use of sanctions as a foreign policy tool.

Chapter 2
Objectives

Sanctions have been imposed in order to pursue multiple, sometimes overlapping, objectives, ranging from signalling the senders resolve to destabilizing countries in pursuit of regime change. This complexity has led scholars to come up with a number of categories under which sanctions objectives can be subsumed. Giumelli (2011), for example, argues that objectives can serve three different objectives: (1) to coerce a target to change its behavior, (2) to constrain the targeted state, and (3) to signal dissatisfaction with a targets behavior or policies. Hufbauer et al. (2007, pp. 52–53) present a slightly different set of categorizations that includes inducing policy change, regime change (by destabilizing the target country), disrupting military operations, and constraining the target country's military capabilities.[1] They also argue that deterrence and punishment can be explicit goals of sanctions, as well as signalling the senders resolve internationally and to a domestic audience (Hufbauer et al., 2007, pp. 5–6).

Similarly, we adopt a categorization of five broad objectives a sanctioner may pursue (see especially Lindsay, 1986; but also Barber, 1979, Hufbauer et al., 2007; Marinov, 2005). The first objective refers to *coercion*. Commonly assumed, states pursue this objective in order to demand that the targeted state undoes something—its policy or behavior —it has already done. The second objective relates to *constrainment*. It has often been seen as damaging a target's economic potential in order to limit its military capabilities (Hufbauer et al., 2007, p. 53). This objective has an explicit material impact and aims at the capabilities states might possess if sanctions had not been implemented. The targeted state should be constrained in its ability to do something, it might have done otherwise. The third objective is *deterrence*. Deterring a target from undertaking an objectionable act is inherently

Supplementary Information The online version contains supplementary material available at https://doi.org/10.1007/978-3-031-17397-4_2.

[1] See also Hufbauer et al. (2007, 66–73) for examples of sanctions regime falling into each category.

different than constraining it. While the latter should limit the target's capabilities, deterrence relates to its resolve. Thus, a conceptual distinction is necessary. As such, the sender threatens other states not to do something or the target not to repeat the objected behavior. The sender aims to undermine the resolve of the target or other states in order to deter future actions (see, e.g., Miller, 2014). The fourth objective pertains to *destabilization*. States have frequently aimed to change the regime or even the political system of unfriendly or hostile counterparts. Marinov (2005) has argued that destabilization may be a necessary condition for successful coercion. Destabilization in this case may be aimed at the government, seeking to create a rift between different elite groups, or it can aim at destabilizing the relationship between the government and the general public. The fifth objective refers to *signalling* and has conceptually been less straightforward. Some scholars argue that signalling can either be directed to a domestic or international audience. Some have considered it to be mere symbolism—doing something, when nothing else can be achieved. We agree with Baldwin's (2000, p. 102) argument that signals are influence attempts. Signalling resolve, a willingness to act, credibility to allies, or a broader *international audience* are attempts to change the recipient's image of the sender (see also Kirshner, 2002, pp. 169–70). These relate, as Barber (1979) put it, to "[...] the status, reputation and position of the government imposing them." (pp. 379–80). However, in our perception, it is equally important to contemplate how the sender attempts to change the image of the target in the eyes of other countries. Broadly speaking, blaming and shaming the target, aiming for its soft power or status in the international system are influence attempts insofar as they affect the position and reputation of the target. As we see it, the punitive aspect of signalling might then be of an immaterial nature to the target. On the other hand, signalling might require the sender to incur costs to appear resolved or as Baldwin (2000) argues "costs are necessary to differentiate a credible signal from 'cheap talk'." (p. 90). We propose a different view on signalling to a *domestic audience*. It has often (if at all) been considered that states implement sanctions to fend off domestic criticism or attain domestic benefits—e.g., an electoral advantage or higher popularity—while its leader might not anticipate to achieve other objectives (Lindsay, 1986, p. 156; Whang, 2011). In our opinion, domestic signalling differs from all other objectives in two significant respects. First, it does neither relate to the target nor to other states but exclusively to its domestic audience. Second, while all other objectives have a punitive aspect in one or the other way, domestic signalling does not. Therefore, we suggest that domestic signalling might be an aspect of other objectives. States implementing sanctions might always have one eye on the target and the other on its constituency. A sender's government, whatever objectives they might seek, want to appear busy, resolved or as acting decisively in times of crisis (Galtung, 1967, p. 411; Barber, 1979, p. 380), either to defend against contenders or simply to capitalize on it. Similarly, we do not include punishment as a separate objective of sanctions (but see also Nossal, 1989). We argue that the punitive aspect is inherent to each of the objectives mentioned above. Sanctions always administer harm in some form onto the perceived wrongdoer or deprive it of some material or immaterial value. The following section will discuss the specific objectives the senders (USA,

UN, and EU) pursue by imposing sanctions in the case of Iran, North Korea, and Russia.

2.1 Iran

US sanctions policy has evolved considerably over time as a result of changes in the security environment in the Middle East as well as due to changes in US strategy and foreign policy objectives. Under both the Clinton and Bush administration sanctions constituted essentially the centerpiece of the US's approach toward Iran, given that the rigid sanctions regime in place curtailed almost all economic and diplomatic interactions between the two countries. Furthermore, US sanctions during this period have been criticized for trying to achieve a too diverse set of goals, ranging from slowing down or stopping Iran's weapons of mass destruction program, inhibiting Iran's support for terrorism, end its aggressive stance against Israel, and stop human rights violations (O'Sullivan, 2010, p. 11). This lack of focus and lack of channels for reengagement put into question if the USA were genuinely seeking to compel Iran to change its behavior or if the USA ultimately just sought to impose costs on a country opposed to the USA for domestic political reasons and to underline the US's international position as the sole remaining superpower. The argument that the USA used sanctions during this time to signal its strength both domestically and internationally rather than seeking to compel Iran is further given credibility by the fact that many experts at the time questioned both the feasibility of achieving the postulated goals and the impact the sanctions were having on the Iranian economy. The question of what the true objectives of US sanctions were, was further complicated by the fact that US officials were ambiguous about if the USA was supporting regime change in Iran (Dumbrell, 2007), increased funding by the US Department of State to groups and channels opposing the Iranian regime (Kessler, 2006) as well as George W. Bush's famous speech including Iran in the "Axis of Evil," a list of rogue states including Iraq and North Korea (Bush, 2002). This ambiguity and failure to clearly articulate a commitment to not interfere in Iran's internal affairs has led some to view the sanctions regime targeting Iran as part of a neo-imperialist US strategy to dominate the region and its strategically important energy reserves (Yazdani & Hussain, 2006). As intentions and true objectives are notoriously hard to identify, a definitive assessment of what the US goal or goals were during this period will have to wait for the declassification of communications inside the US government. From a security and foreign policy perspective, the USA should have a clear preference for a change in the Iranian regime compared to a continued hostile relationship with the Iranian government. Nonetheless, it remains unclear if the US government ever considered it to be a feasible outcome of its sanctions policy rather than just an unintentional, albeit potentially welcomed, consequence. Some statements, including for example, President Bush's State of the Union Address in January 2006 expressing hopes to "be the closest of friends with a free and democratic Iran" (Bush, 2006), suggest that regime change was an option considered by the administration. However, support to the domestic opposition in Iran or military action appears to have been the options considered for regime change, while sanctions were not considered to be a viable tool to achieve this goal (Cooper & Sanger, 2007). While there have been modest efforts to strengthen the domestic opposition (Kessler, 2006) and continued calls for military action from outside the administration, the USA seemed to slowly start to put a bigger focus on using sanctions to address the Iranian nuclear issue in 2006 through multilateral diplomacy, including through UN sanctions and by joining the EU-Iran talks.

However, only with the start of the Presidency of Barack Obama, the USA made the nuclear issue its central focus of engagement with Iran. In addition to focusing on addressing the Iranian nuclear issue through expanding the multilateral sanctions regime at the UN to increase pressure on Iran, the US government was seeking engagement with the Iranian leadership in order to seek a diplomatic resolution to the nuclear issue (Jin, 2010). This appears to reflect the recognition that the objectives of sanctions during the Clinton and Bush presidencies were too broad that an unilateral approach to sanctions was not effective enough and that increased pressure had to be accompanied by channels and diplomatic exchanges that allow for rapprochement between the USA and Iran (see, e.g., O'Sullivan, 2010). This does not mean that sanctions in other areas, including in response to human rights violations, were ignored, but were mostly imposed for the purpose of continuing to show that such behavior was not acceptable. This narrower focus on finding a diplomatic solution to ensuring the solely civilian purpose of Iran's nuclear program and using sanctions relief as an incentive for Iran to engage in negotiations ultimately seemed to have been successful, as Iran and the P5 + 1 (or EU3 + 3) were able to agree on adopting the Joint Comprehensive Plan of Action (JCPOA) that puts temporary but rigorous restrictions on Iran's nuclear program in return for the easing of UN, EU, and US sanctions.[2]

Notably, while many observers touted the Iranian nuclear deal a success of multilateral diplomacy as well as underlined the important role sanctions had played in bringing Iran to the negotiation table, the deal also received much criticism from the beginning. Support inside the USA was also relatively weak, with the Republicans partly strictly opposing it. So it came with little surprise when after Donald Trump was elected as President, that voices inside the US government advocating that the USA should unilaterally leave the JCPOA and reimpose sanctions became stronger, culminating in President Trump announcing in May 2018 the US withdrawal from the deal (Landler, 2018). After the US withdrawal, the Trump administration imposed a strategy of "maximum pressure" against Iran that according to US Secretary of State Mike Pompeo consisted of "diplomatic isolation, economic pressure, and military deterrence" in order to restore the credibility of US threats and

---

[2] For a discussion on the rationale behind using both pressure and incentives during diplomatic engagement, see, e.g., Dorussen (2001). It also has to be noted that the change in US policy towards Iran was not the only factor in making the JCPOA possible, albeit probably one of the most important ones.

signalling its resolve (Pompeo, 2020). The objectives of new campaign of "maximum pressure" were also much broader than the Obama administration's narrow focus on finding a negotiated solution to the Iranian nuclear issue. Again, as under the Clinton and Bush presidency, the purpose of US sanctions was to address a wide range of issues by imposing costs on Iran to stop its nuclear weapons program, missile development, support for terrorist organizations, and inimical regional policies that undermine peace and security in the Middle East (Pompeo, 2018). In addition to trying to compel Iran from changing its behavior in these areas and deterring Iran from engaging in further dangerous behavior, the USA has also signalled its interest in finding a new, broader, negotiated settlement with Iran.[3] Furthermore, while the Trump administration never indicated it directly, some critics of President Trump's maximum pressure strategy have argued that the strategy was designed to fail, by demanding unrealistic concessions from Iran, and that the administrations real objective was to destabilize the Iranian regime in order to make regime change a possibility (Rover, 2020). However, as already discussed above, it is difficult to discern if regime change was an actual objective pursued by the US government.

Textbox 1: List of US Demands to Iran (2018)
U.S. Secretary of State Mike Pompeo outlined 12 basic requirements for a new agreement with Iran on nuclear and regional issues

1. Iran must provide a complete account of its previous nuclear-weapons research.
2. Iran must stop uranium enrichment and never pursue plutonium reprocessing.
3. Iran must provide the International Atomic Energy Agency "unqualified access" to all sites in the country.
4. Iran must stop providing missiles to militant groups and halt the development of nuclear-capable missiles.
5. Iran must release all US and allied detainees.
6. Iran must stop supporting militant groups, including Hezbollah, Hamas, and Palestinian Islamic Jihad.
7. Iran must respect Iraqi sovereignty and permit the demobilization of the Shiite militias it has backed there.
8. Iran must stop sending arms to the Houthis and work for a peaceful settlement in Yemen.
9. Iran must withdraw all forces under its command from Syria.

(continued)

---

[3] See Textbox 1: List of US demands to Iran (2018) for the full set of basic requirements Pompeo laid out in his speech Gordon (2018).

> **Textbox 1** (continued)
> 10. Iran must end support for the Taliban and stop harboring al Qaeda militants.
> 11. Iran must end support by its paramilitary Quds Force for militant groups.
> 12. Iran must end its threats to destroy Israel and stop threatening international ships. It must end cyberattacks and stop proxies from firing missiles into Saudi Arabia and the United Arab Emirates.

In contrast to the USA, and as described above, the EU only emerged as a more relevant sanctioning actor after 2006, when the UN Security Council imposed its first round of sanctions against Iran. However, the EU's efforts focused mostly on passing legislation aimed at implementing UN sanctions, and only in 2010, the EU started to supplement them with its own autonomous restrictive measures. The EU's evolution to becoming a more proactive sanctioning actor reflects a number of developments in Iran, inside the EU itself as well as concerning relations with the USA. The EU's engagement with Iran in the early 2000s was driven by an objective to improve relations with Iran through negotiations led by the United Kingdom, France, and Germany (E-3). While the EU's diplomatic approach was able to produce some successes during this period, most notably the 2004 Paris Agreement, where Iran agreed to halt uranium enrichment and committed to implement the IAEA's Additional Protocol, it ultimately was not able to resolve the nuclear issue (Portela, 2015). This failure, coupled with the more hawkish stance of the newly elected Iranian President Mahmoud Ahmadinejad, gradually led the UK, France, and Germany to take on a harder stance toward Iran. Furthermore, the EU started to increasingly view the Iranian nuclear program to pose a real threat to peace and stability in the region by either provoking a nuclear arms race or by incentivizing Israel and/or the USA to take military action against Iran (Patterson, 2013, p. 138). This reflects an acknowledgment by the EU that in order to achieve a "comprehensive, negotiated, long-term settlement" with Iran on its nuclear issue it had to adopt a dual track approach combining engagement with pressure (EEAS, 2013, p. 1). In this regard, the objective of EU sanctions was to increase the pressure on Iran to resume a constructive engagement with the P5 + 1 and to persuade "Iran to comply with its international obligations and to constrain its development of sensitive technologies in support of its nuclear and missile programmes" (EEAS, 2013, p. 2).

Similarly to the views of the UK, France, and Germany being decisive for EU sanction policy (see, e.g., Patterson, 2013, p. 141), the permanent five members of the UN Security Council are essential for the UN adopting sanctions. Given that UN Security Council resolutions and positions often reflect the lowest common denominator between the five permanent members and as the objectives of the USA and the EU were discussed above, the objectives of the remaining two permanent members, China and Russia, will be focused on here. The Chinese approach was mostly defined by an interest in preventing a nuclear-armed Iran through a diplomatic

2.1 Iran

solution, while ensuring that neither the USA nor Israel chose to take military actions against Iran which would jeopardize Chinese economic interests in the region, including its energy trade and ambitious One Belt One Road project (Garver, 2016). Furthermore, China for a long time had expressed its opposition to the use of sanctions to resolve the issue (Quan, 2006), as also highlighted by Chinese Foreign Ministry spokesman Hong Lei who reiterated that "sanctions are not the correct way to ease tensions or resolve the issue of Iran's nuclear program [...] The correct path is dialogue and negotiations" (Blanchard, 2012). Nonetheless, China did not use its veto rights in the UN Security Council to prevent the four UN Security Council resolutions that imposed sanctions against Iran between 2006 and 2009, indicating the importance China places on being a reliable actor in international efforts to prevent nuclear proliferation. Hence, finding a solution to the issue through a negotiated settlement, like the JCPOA, has been in China's interest, further underlined by China's continued commitment to the JCPOA even after the US withdrawal from the agreement. The approach Russia has taken toward the Iranian nuclear issue appears to be very similar to the Chinese approach. This is not surprising given the shared position against "Western" unilateralism as well as the importance both China and Russia place with regard to opposing notions of regime change and intervening in the internal affairs of sovereign states. As China, Russia also continuously opposed using sanctions against Iran, however, proposed a more nuanced argument by highlighting the possibility that sanctions could be considered as part of a diplomatic-negotiated approach to solving the issue (Lavrov, 2005; Medvedev, 2010). This approach has also been driven by an interest by Russia to avoid a nuclear-armed Iran that could provoke escalatory dynamics in the region with Israel or Saudi Arabia, while ensuring states' rights to the development of nuclear energy for civilian purposes. Furthermore, supporting limited UN sanctions against Iran can be viewed as an attempt to decrease the likelihood of US or Israeli military intervention in Iran that would destabilize the region, while also trying to retain relatively good relationships with Iran.[4] In addition, Russia, as China, wants to be viewed as committed and responsible actor on international efforts to prevent the proliferation of WMDs, as well as being supporters of international law and of the UN Security Council as the central institution to solve matters that threaten international peace and security. As mentioned above, the UN Security Council resolutions reflect these differing positions and objectives pursued by the permanent members. Hence, when the UN Security Council started to impose sanctions on Iran in 2006 it reflects the hardening stance of France and the UK, as well as the shifting assessment by China and Russia of a potential escalation. The absence of new UN sanctions in the 2010s also mirrors the Chinese and Russian balancing act between appeasing the USA while protecting their own interests, both economic and diplomatic, in the region.

---

[4]Russian officials often caution about the use of sanctions and military intervention, particularly, when not mandated by the UNSC, by highlighting the experience of the USA during the 2003 Iraq invasion (Lavrov, 2005).

2.2 North Korea

The international sanctions regime against North Korea follows similar objectives as the measures taken with regard to the Iranian nuclear issue. The measures in a broad sense aim to constrain North Korea by limiting its access to materials needed for its nuclear weapons program, imposing costs on the North Korean leadership by inhibiting trade and access to luxury goods, isolating North Korea economically to restrict its financial and material resources to advance its nuclear and ballistic missile programs and increase diplomatic pressure. Combined these objectives are aimed at slowing down North Korean progress on its nuclear and ballistic missile programs, seeking to deter its aggressive and provocative behavior and pressuring North Korea to find a negotiated solution (preferably in the format of the six-party talks[5]) to the denuclearization of North Korea. As EU and US objectives will be discussed in more detail below, the initial focus of this section will be on the two other permanent members of the UN Security Council, China, and Russia. As with Iran, neither China nor Russia has an interest in a nuclear-armed North Korea. Both countries are wary of how this could spur nuclear proliferation in the region as well as how this could prompt the USA to ramp up its military presence in the region. Furthermore, China in particular is concerned about the negative impact a military escalation on the Korean Peninsula could have, with the potential of large numbers of refugees seeking shelter in China. However, while China is wary of the negative ramifications, it is also concerned about potential regime collapse or what a potential diplomatic solution to the situation on the Korean Peninsula could look like. Particularly, China worries that a unified Korea could mean that the USA can extend its military presence, which is currently limited to South Korea, to the whole peninsula and to the Chinese-Korean border, therefore losing its "buffer zone" to the USA (Mangott & Senn, 2017; Nanto & Manyin, 2010). Hence, China's primary objective with regard to its sanctions policy has been to preserve stability and avoid a North Korean regime collapse, while still being seen as an important part of multilateral efforts to prevent the proliferation of nuclear weapons. Russia shares a similar interest, although compared with China, for Russia, the stakes are not as high. In this regard, Russia has adopted a similar set of objectives toward North Korea. It aims at constraining North Koreas nuclear ambitions through UN Security Council sanctions and a revitalization of the six-party talks, while avoiding the harshest of sanctions in order to preserve the stability on the Korean Peninsula and not risk a collapse of the North Korean regime. Russia has also expressed its strong opposition to using the situation on the Korean Peninsula to enhance US and US allies military capacities in the region (UN Security Council, 2016). It has further called for restraining sanctions in order not to harm the "economy of the Democratic People's

---

[5]The six-party talks used to be the main format in which multilateral negotiations around the resolution of North Korea's nuclear weapons program were held. Participants included China, Japan, North Korea, South Korea, Russia, and the USA. A number of talks were held between 2003 and 2007, however, the format was discontinued after North Korea left the format in April 2009.

2.2 North Korea

Republic of Korea and to exacerbate the country's humanitarian situation" (see, e.g., the Russian UN representative at the meeting of the UN Security Council, 2016). In addition to these objectives, Russia has in recent years sought to improve its economic relationship, particularly infrastructure development, with North Korea. This has further amplified Russia's interest in avoiding the strictest of sanctions against the country (Mangott & Senn, 2017, p. 20).

The EU's sanctions policy is closely aligned with multilateral efforts at the UN. In this regard, the EU is regularly transposing and implementing relevant UN resolutions against North Korea's nuclear and ballistic weapons program. Furthermore, the EU is complementing UN measures with its own autonomous restrictive measures. Given how EU measures are closely aligned with UN sanctions and the very limited role the EU plays economically for North Korea, its sanctions policy does closely reflect the objectives pursued by the UN. This is exemplified by the EU's approach of "Critical Engagement" toward North Korea. Its objective is to achieve the "complete, verifiable and irreversible denuclearization of the Korean Peninsula" through a diplomatic process (Council of the European Union, 2019a), complemented by exerting pressure on the regime through UN and autonomous EU sanctions.

Much more so than the EU, the USA plays a central role with regard to the developments on the Korean Peninsula and it uses its sanctions regime against North Korea to address a wide range of, in US terms, objectionable activities. In addition to its nuclear and ballistic missile programs, the sanctions are seeking to address North Korea's activities that cause regional disruptions, its involvement in narcotics trafficking, its undemocratic governance, and its illicit activities in international markets (Rennack, 2020, p. 1). While sanctions were imposed for this wide range of issues, their central purpose was to increase pressure on North Korea to find a diplomatic solution to its nuclear weapons program. Sanctions became an increasingly important tool after the six-party talks all but failed in 2009, which prompted the Obama administration to increase the pressure on North Korea through unilateral and multilateral sanctions. The Obama administration's approach for most of his presidency was characterized by a policy of "strategic patience," which centered on escalating pressure on North Korea but at the same time expressing the conditional willingness to engage in negotiations if North Korea showed serious commitment. With Trump assuming office in 2017, the USA adopted a strategy of "maximum pressure," similar to the one against Iran, which introduced a series of additional sanctions, including some UN sanctions resolutions, in order to block additional North Korean revenue sources as well as its import of fuel and other commodities. In addition to sanctions pressure, the Trump administration emphasized US openness to negotiations and high-ranking US officials even publicly stated that the US's goal was not to seek regime change (Mattis & Tillerson, 2017). However, in contrast to the Obama administration, and revealing tensions inside the US administrations, the Trump administration also publicly discussed the possibilities of a preventive military strike against North Korea (Sciutto & Bash, 2018). This approach of increasing pressure, signalling openness to diplomatic engagement but also highlighting the possibility of a military option, interrupted by some episodes of escalatory rhetoric,[6] seemed to have some success in promoting diplomatic engagement between the two countries and resulted in the first official meeting between a US president and its North Korean counterpart. However, these efforts so far have not yet developed into tangible progress with regard to the US's objective of achieving the denuclearization of the Korean Peninsula.

2.3 Russia

In response to Russia's annexation of Crimea in 2014 and its involvement in the conflict in Eastern Ukraine, the EU has imposed multiple stages of sanctions against Russia that have seen an expansion in scope targeting companies, entities, and persons associated with the Russian government (the newest sanctions following the Russian invasion of Ukraine will be discussed in the section on Recent Developments). The first set of sanctions was mostly symbolic in nature, imposing travel bans and asset freezes on officials and the persons and entities associated with them for their role in threatening "the territorial integrity, sovereignty and independence of Ukraine" (Council of the European Union, 2014). This first round of sanctions also included a number of political and diplomatic measures, such as cancelling the bilateral summits with Russia and suspending G8 Summit preparations. Supplementing its sanctions imposition, the EU from the start of the crisis articulated its interest in finding a peaceful settlement but also underlined its commitment to imposing additional restrictive measures if the conflict parties would fail to make progress or further escalate the situation. After initial attempts to de-escalate the situation had failed, the EU introduced a first set of four steps[7] to be taken by Russia in order to avoid the adoption of stronger and more comprehensive sanctions against Russia. This step, linking the adoption of additional restrictive measures to the success or failure to take concrete actions was characteristic of the EU's approach to the Ukraine crisis. This dual track approach of the EU of imposing sanctions on Russia while seeking to engage Russia diplomatically in bilateral as well as multilateral formats aimed at compelling Russia to "reverse the annexation of Crimea and Sevastopol, prevent supplies, arms and illegal fighters crossing the border to Ukraine, and use its influence to persuade the rebels in Donetsk and Lugansk to back down" (Fischer, 2015, p. 2). More concretely, in March 2015, the European Council decided to align the economic sanctions regime against Russia to the full

---

[6] E.g., US President Trumps threat to bring fire and fury to North Korea if it continued to threaten the USA, or North Koreas official announcement that it was considering conducting an atmospheric nuclear test Wertz (2018, 16).

[7] The four steps include: an agreement on a verification mechanism through the OSCE, a cease-fire and border control; return of Ukrainian border checkpoints; the release of hostages; and initiating negotiations on implementing a peace plan.

2.3 Russia

implementation of the Minsk agreements,[8] noting that economic sanctions would be extended, if the agreements were not fully implemented by December 31, 2015. Given that the Minsk agreements have not been fully implemented, the EU continued its approach of regularly extending the duration of its economic sanctions. Therefore, the EU continued to constrain Russia by limiting its access to the EU financial markets for a number of select financial, defense, and energy companies, banning arms trade, banning the export of dual-use goods, and limiting its access to technologies used for oil production and exploration. In addition, the sanctions imposed against persons and entities involved in actions undermining the territorial integrity of Ukraine is regularly extended and updated (Council of the European Union, 2019b, 2020).The US and EU sanctions regimes in response to the crisis in Ukraine had initially been developed in close coordination. Therefore, and particularly with regard to sanctions targeting the financial, defense, and energy sector, the sanction measures imposed by the USA and the EU against Russia mirror each other in many ways. Particularly at the beginning of the crisis, US and EU objectives and measures were closely aligned. The sanctions imposed were intended to inflict costs on Russia for its actions in Ukraine in order to deter further aggressions and incentivize diplomatic steps to de-escalate the crisis. Costs were mostly targeted at Russia's energy sector, Russia's central revenue source, and against individuals that were deemed to be involved in the actions in Ukraine or persons being close to the inner circle of the Russian government. Nonetheless, there are some notable differences when it comes to the goals that the USA is trying to achieve by imposing its sanctions regime. While the EU was always careful to avoid sanctions that could negatively impact some of its member states that are heavily reliant on the Russian energy supply, the USA has taken actions that could end up harming some EU member states economically (Blanc & Weiss, 2019). In addition, while the sanctions regimes (initially) had been coordinated closely, this mostly applied to sanctions with regard to Russian actions in Crimea and Eastern Ukraine. Not only has the USA imposed sanctions against Russia for a number of additional actions, like cyber-activities, Russia's involvement in the Syrian civil war or corruption, but in recent years EU and US interests on the Ukrainian issue had diverged further. The most apparent of which are the US sanctions against the Russian energy export projects Nord Stream and TurkStream, which the EU strongly opposed (European Commission, 2021). What furthermore differentiates EU from US sanctions is the fact that the EU has clearly linked sanctions relief to the implementation of the Minsk agreements. While US officials during the Obama administration had repeatedly stated that if Russia played its part in implementing the Minsk agreements, it could result in the lifting of sanctions (Martin, 2016), the Trump administration did not reiterate this possibility. That the USA did not make it a central piece of its sanctions

---

[8]The measures agreed on in the Minsk Protocol from September 5, 2014 can be found at https://peacemaker.un.org/sites/peacemaker.un.org/files/UA_140905_MinskCeasfire_en.pdf and additional measures agreed to on February 12, 2015 can be found at https://peacemaker.un.org/sites/peacemaker.un.org/files/UA_150212_MinskAgreement_en.pdf

policy to link the implementation of the Minsk agreements to sanctions relief, made it ambiguous for Russian officials what steps to take in order to reduce US sanctions, which in turn decreases the likelihood of sanctions producing their intended effects. These diverging interests have however aligned once again following the war in Ukraine. Both the USA and the EU want to hold Russia accountable for its unlawful actions by imposing severe economic and political costs on the Russian government and Russian elites. Both sides have made it clear that there will be no sanctions relief without de-escalation and restoration of Ukraine's sovereignty (European Commission, 2022a; The White House Briefing Room, 2022c).

Chapter 3
Measures

Most studies investigating sanctions either analyze sanctions at the sanctions regime or sanction episode level. At the sanctions regime level this means essentially grouping multiple individual sanctions measures together depending on the target or the type of behavior.[1] On the other hand, studies have tried to identify time periods that correspond to coherent sanctions episodes, with the end of a sanctions period mostly defined by either the termination of relevant sanctions or significant changes in the senders' objectives (e.g., a change from a simple change in behavior to regime change). This study, however, seeks to adopt a different approach. Instead of aggregating measures, measures are treated as individual events, with their own respective objectives and effects. Such an approach allows for a more nuanced understanding of the tactics of sanctions imposition—when, why, and how states and international organizations impose sanctions—while allowing to take into account the larger strategic environment in which all international actors operate.

Therefore, this section will start by giving an overview of the variety of measures and their provisions imposed by the United Nations, the European Union, and the USA. The section below will first give an overview over general trends in sanctions imposition in the three aforementioned cases and provide a broader historical context before exploring more recent sanction measures in more detail. This section is structured by target country and grouped by function and in chronological order in which they had been imposed.

All sanctions measures discussed in this section are listed in the Appendix, including web links to the original documents and short narrative summaries.

Supplementary Information The online version contains supplementary material available at https://doi.org/10.1007/978-3-031-17397-4_3.

---

[1] Examples for this include the United Nations sanction regimes against states like South Africa, Iraq or Liberia, but also more recently against terrorist organizations such as ISIL/ISIS and Al-Qaida.

3.1 Trends in Sanctions Imposition

There are a number of general trends that can be observed when it comes to the use of sanctions by the UN, the EU, and the USA. First, sanctions have become increasingly important as a foreign policy tool for each of the three actors mentioned above over the course of the last three decades. For the USA, this trend of increasingly employing sanctions is relatively constant and continuous since at least the imposition of sanctions against the Islamic Republic of Iran in 1979 as a response to the Islamic Revolution that resulted in the overthrow of the government led by the Shah of Iran, a close US ally in the Middle East.

The use of sanctions as a primary foreign policy tool by the EU in contrast is more recent. While the EU had started to impose sanctions autonomously in the early 1980s, a structured approach only really took shape in the early 1990s after the adoption of the EU's Common Foreign and Security Policy (CFSP) and increased in sophistication when the EU's Political and Security Committee agreed on basic principles and guidelines on the implementation of sanctions in 2004 (Portela, 2005). This trend has continued to increase ever since, making sanctions (or "restrictive measures" as sanctions are referred to by the EU) an integral part in promoting its CFSP goals.

In comparison, the sanctions imposition trend for the UN has not been as constant. After decades of gridlock between the USA and the Soviet Union had severely limited the decision-making ability of the UN Security Council (UNSC), the dissolution of the Soviet Union and the end of the Cold War allowed the UN to take a more proactive role in international relations. This also allowed the UNSC to pass multiple sanctions in the 1990s and early 2000s and making the UN a central actor in the international sanctions arena. However, in recent years, due to deteriorating relations, between the USA and Russia in particular, and with China taking a more assertive role in the UNSC, passing of additional sanctions resolutions is predicted to become increasingly difficult (Morgan et al., 2014). Nonetheless, with the rise of non-conventional threats to international security, including transnational terrorist groups and criminal organizations, the UN has managed to position itself as a central actor in coordinating multilateral responses, including via sanctions, to these threats.

In addition to sanctions having become a more prevalent foreign policy instrument, there have been efforts to increase the precision of sanctions, which has resulted in the imposition of the so-called targeted or smart sanctions (see, e.g., Drezner, 2011, 2015; Portela, 2016; Wallensteen & Grusell, 2012). However, while this has not resulted in the abandonment of broad economic sanctions or arms embargoes (comprehensive sanctions), targeted sanctions are increasingly used to complement or in some circumstances to substitute them. This development can be attributed to the recognition that elites in target countries can often avert the costs of broad economic sanctions to some degree and that it is the general population that suffers most from sanctions. Furthermore, in many of the most oppressive countries, the ability of the general population to exert pressure on its government is very limited. In line with Selectorate Theory, a prominent theory of leadership survival in autocratic regimes, nondemocratic regimes depend on a select few for legitimacy and power rather than on the general population (Bueno de Mesquita, 2005).[2] Hence, according to the logic of targeted sanctions, imposing costs on select few elites that are close to the state leadership and reducing their liberties should be more effective in exerting pressure on regimes to change their behavior.

3.2 Iran

While Iran has been subject to multiple sanctions measures since its inception in 1979, in particular by the USA, the UN only started imposing sanctions in response to concerns that Iran may pursue a clandestine nuclear weapons program. The UN Security Council first imposed sanctions against Iran in 2006, following a report by the International Atomic Energy Agency (IAEA) finding Iran to be in noncompliance with its Non-Proliferation Treaty (NPT) Safeguards Agreement commitments (IAEA, 2006). After Iran had failed to comply with UN Security Council resolution 1696 (2006) to suspend nuclear enrichment and reprocessing activities, the Security Council passed resolution 1737 (2006), resolution 1747 (2007), resolution 1803 (2008), resolution 1835 (2008) and resolution 1929 (2010). Resolutions 1737, 1747, 1803, and 1929 were passed by the Security Council, in its role as the leading UN body to maintain international peace and security and under Article 41 of Chapter VII of the UN Charter. The resolutions include sanctions to prevent Iran from acquiring nuclear and ballistic missile-related goods, freezing funds and assets of individuals and entities engaged in activities related to Iran's nuclear or ballistic missile program and limiting the arms sales from and to Iran. Resolution 1835 was not passed under Article 41 of Chapter VII and did not include new sanctions measures; however, the resolution expressed the Security Council's commitment to a diplomatic and negotiated settlement of the Iranian nuclear issue.

Following the P5 + 1 (the permanent five Security Council members[3] and Germany) reaching an agreement with Iran on the nuclear issue in July 2015, also known as the Joint Comprehensive Plan of Action (JCPOA), the UN Security Council passed resolution 2231 (2015) supporting the agreement. Most notably, resolution 2231 terminated all previous UN resolutions related to the Iranian nuclear program on January 16, 2016, the Implementation Day of the JCPOA. It further

---

[2] This does not imply that autocratic leaders cannot be held accountable domestically. Weeks (2008) argues that nondemocratic regimes leaders can indeed be held accountable by domestic political groups, depending on their ability to coordinate to punish their leader.

[3] The permanent members of the Security Council are China, France, Russia, the United Kingdom, and the USA.

provided for a sequential lifting of the arms embargo on Iran after 5 years and the ballistic missile-related sanctions after 8 years.[4]

In line with the JCPOA, the European Union lifted most of its sanctions against Iran during the Implementation Phase. However, prior to the agreement between the P5 + 1 and Iran, the EU had imposed wide-ranging sanctions. In addition to implementing UN resolutions 1737, 1747, 1803, and 1929 through EU Council legislation,[5] the European Union had adopted a number of restrictive financial and economic measures autonomously from the UN. Autonomous EU sanctions included extensive restrictions on imports and exports to and from Iran.[6] These restrictions included a ban on exporting arms, dual-use items and goods that could be used in the process of nuclear enrichment to Iran. The sanctions also restricted EU member states' trade with Iran's energy sector, one of the central sources of revenue for the Iranian government, including crude oil, natural gas, petroleum products, and technical equipment essential for the energy sector. The EU also took measures targeting the Iranian financial sector. This included freezing the assets of Iran's major state-owned and commercial banks and even encompassed the Iranian Central Bank which got listed on 23 January 2012 by the EU due to its involvement in circumventing sanctions and providing financial support to the Iranian regime. As part of the EU's strategy to prevent Iran from acquiring goods, financial resources and technology that could support a military nuclear program, the EU also restricted the Iranian transportation sector as well as travel for listed persons. Finally, EU measures also include a ban on trading gold, other precious metals, and diamonds with Iran.

As discussed above, these measures were all lifted during the implementation of the JCPOA. However, a number of restrictions still apply for EU member states when dealing with Iran. These measures remained in place despite the JCPOA, mostly due to the fact that they had been imposed in response to human rights abuses and for support of terrorist organizations. Sanctions still in place include an arms embargo and restrictions on ballistic missile-related technology and materials. A number of Iranian persons and entities also remained under a travel ban or an asset freeze due to their involvement in human rights abuses or their support for terrorism. Sensitive nuclear proliferation related technologies and goods can be supplied to Iran after a prior authorization through the procurement channel setup by the JCPOA.

The United States' sanctions measures are even more expansive than the measures taken by both the UN and the EU, making it the most comprehensive sanctions regime in history. While some of the restrictions had been eased during the implementation of the JCPOA, most of them have been reapplied and new measures have

---

[4] The UN arms embargo ended in October 2020.

[5] See Council Common Position 2007/140/CFSP of 27 February 2007 concerning restrictive measures against Iran and its amendments. The consolidated version can be found at http://data.europa.eu/eli/compos/2007/140/2009-11-17

[6] See Council Decision 2010/413/CFSP of 26 July 2010 and its amendments, most notably Council Decision 2012/635/CFSP of 15 October 2012.

been added following the US withdrawal from the agreement in May 2018. These renewed sanctions are stated to pressure Iran into negotiating a new agreement that is not only focused on its nuclear weapons program but also addresses a broader range of "malign" Iranian behavior, including its ballistic missile program and its involvement in regional crises (Landler, 2018).

These latest sanctions are only the newest iteration of the USA applying this tool to compel Iran into changing its behavior. The USA has applied economic sanctions against Iran since its inception in 1979 after the Islamic Revolution toppled the incumbent Shah, a close US ally in the Middle East, and the US embassy hostage crisis in Teheran. In response to these events, the first round of sanctions included an almost complete freezing of Iranian assets in the USA and blocking Iranian government property in the USA (Executive Order (E.O.) 12170 of 14 November 1979) and a comprehensive trade ban (E.O. 12205 of 7 April 1980 and E.O. 12211 of 17 April 1980).[7] However, a number of Iranian assets are still frozen, most notably under E.O. 13599 issued on 5 February 2012, which freezes all assets of entities related to the Iranian regime. Most of these entities were removed from the US sanctions list as part of the JCPOA, however, following the unilateral decision of the USA to withdraw from the agreement, these entities were relisted in November 2018. As noted above, the USA had issued a trade ban with Iran in 1980 which got lifted a year later. However, US President Bill Clinton reimposed a ban on US trade with and investment in Iran in 1995. These measures (E.O. 12957 of March 1995 and E.O. 12959 of May 1995) came in response to US suspicions that Iran was pursuing a military nuclear program and Iran's involvement in supporting terrorist groups threatening peace in the Middle East and particularly Israel's security (Perdum, 1995). The ban on trade with Iran was further codified in the Iran Freedom Support Act of 2006 and in the Comprehensive Iran Sanctions, Accountability and Divestment Act of 2010 (CISADA). During the time the USA was part of the JCPOA some restrictions on trade regarding luxury goods were removed but after the US withdrawal this was reversed in August 2018.

Another central aspect of US sanctions policy regarding Iran are its sanctions against Iran's energy sector. The Iran Sanctions Act (ISA) enacted in 1996[8] and subsequent legislation amending it provide a broad set of different sanction measures to be applied to persons and entities that engage in transactions with the Iranian energy sector. If an entity is found to violate the provisions, ISA requires the imposition of at least 5 out of 12 sanctions.[9] ISA provides that entities be sanctioned if they invest more than $20 million in 1 year in Iran's energy sector, particularly into the development of Iran's oil or gas fields. It further applied to entities engaged in the sale or supply of WMD related technologies and advanced conventional weapons

---

[7] The trade ban was lifted by E.O. 12282 (1981) following the Algeria Declaration (Algiers Acoords).

[8] Previously the Iran and Libya Sanctions Act it was renamed in 2006 after it was terminated with regard to Libya.

[9] See Katzman (2020, 16–17).

(added by the Iran Freedom Support Act of 2006) as well as engagement in the uranium mining (added by the Iran Threat Reduction and Syrian Hum Rights Act of 2012, short ITRSHRA). CISADA added provisions for sanctions to be imposed on entities that sell gasoline to Iran. These three legislations together, complemented by E.O. 13622 (2012) and 13846 (2018), cover almost all aspects related to Iran's energy sector, including equipment, transportation, financial investments, and the purchase of Iranian crude oil and related products. Furthermore, the National Defense Authorization Act for 2012 (signed in December 2011) sought to limit Iranian oil exports by imposing sanctions on financial transactions to Iran's banks in order to purchase oil. The USA also has in place sanctions that aim to limit Iran's ability to acquire goods and technology related to the development of weapons of mass destruction, ballistic missiles as well as conventional arms. These measures are generally understood to seek to contain Iran's power and limit its position as a player in the Middle East. The sanctions are provided by several executive orders and laws, most notably the Iran-Iraq Arms Nonproliferation Act (1990), the Iran-North Korea-Syria Nonproliferation Act (2000), E.O. 13382 (2005), and finally the Countering America's Adversaries through Sanctions Act of 2017 (CAATSA). As mentioned above, addressing Iran's support of terrorist organizations and other armed groups through sanctions has been an important part of US relations with Iran. This dates back to 1984 when the USA designated Iran as a state sponsor of terrorism, which in turn triggered a number of sanctions. These sanctions include restrictions on dual-use goods and technology, ban on financial assistance and an arms embargo, restrictions on multilateral lendings and withholding assistance to countries and organizations that assist Iran. The USA has also sanctioned organizations and persons for their support to terrorism under E.O. 13224 (2001) and has designated a number of organizations, that are either part of the Iranian regime or are supported by Iran, as terrorist organizations. This includes the Islamic Revolutionary Guard Corps (IRGC), Hezbollah, and Hamas among others. The development of sanctions against Iran is portrayed in the following diagrams (Figs. 3.1, 3.2 and 3.3).

3.3 North Korea

The primary focus of the current international sanctions regime against the Democratic People's Republic of Korea (DPRK) is in response to the DPRK's nuclear weapons and ballistic missile programs which the regime continues to pursue despite continued UN, EU, and US sanctions.[10] All three sanctions imposing actors maintain that their central objective is to prevent North Korea from continuing its nuclear weapon and ballistic missile program, by preventing North Korea from acquiring material and technology needed, increase costs on the North Korean regime to

---

[10]Previously North Korea had been subject to international sanctions over its aggressions and hostilities during the Korean War.

3.3 North Korea

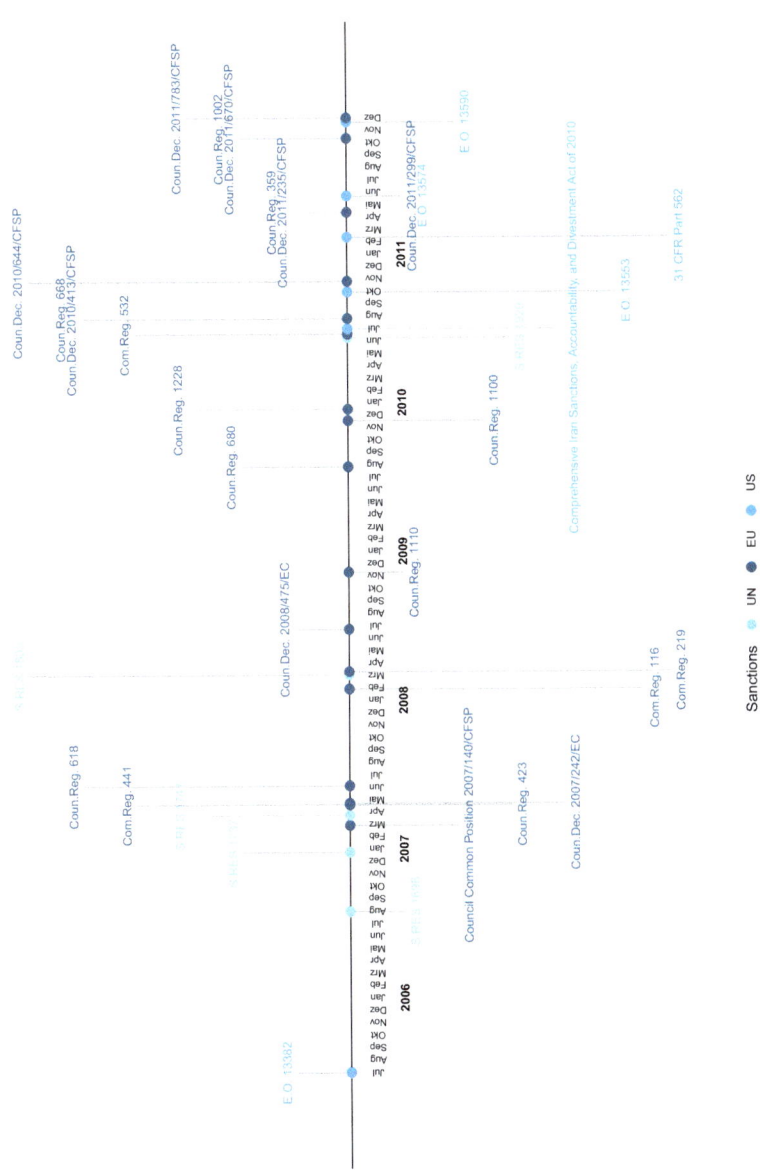

Fig. 3.1 Sanctions against Iran between 2005 and 2012

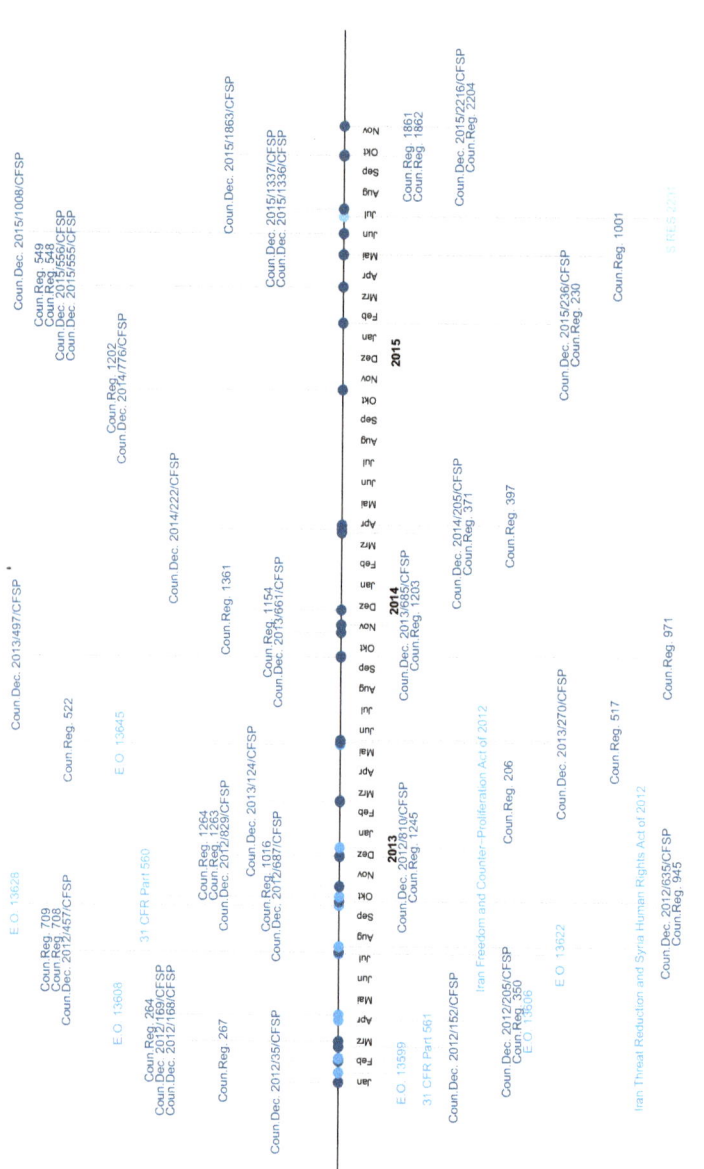

Fig. 3.2 Sanctions against Iran between 2012 and 2016

3.3 North Korea

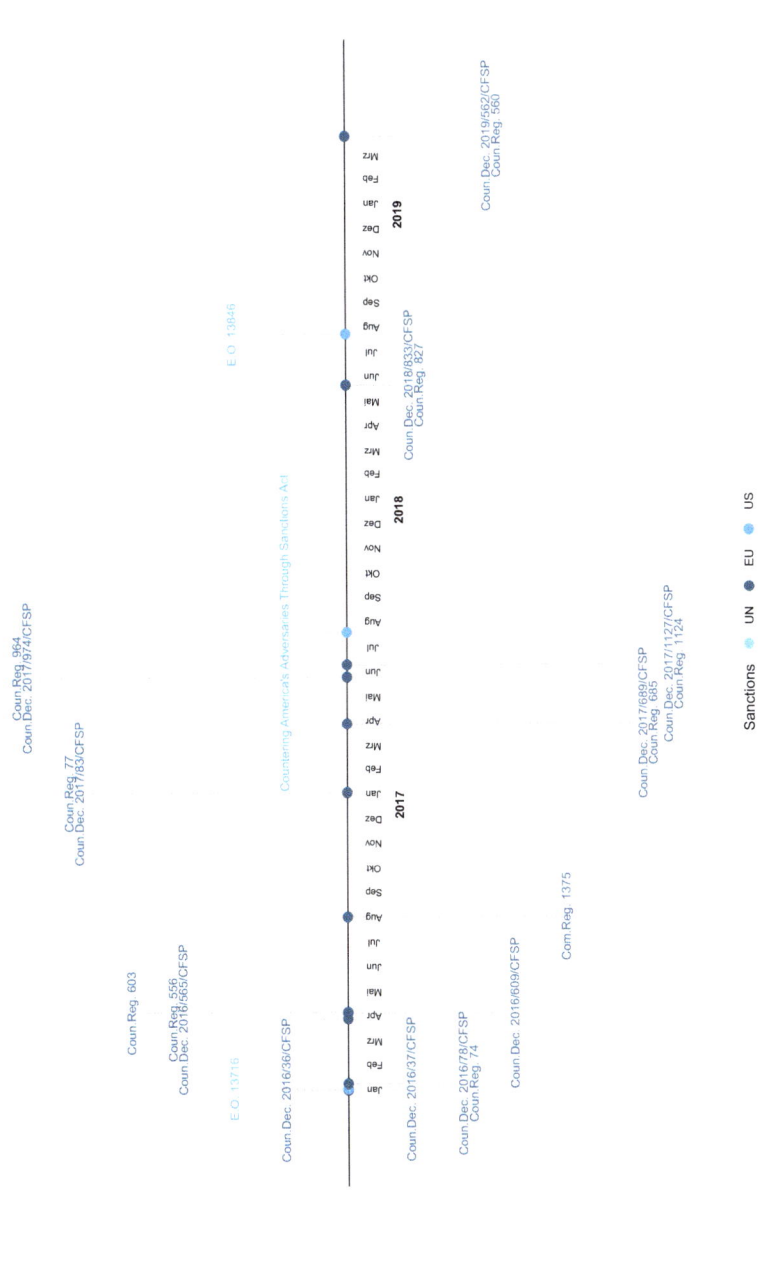

Fig. 3.3 Sanctions against Iran after 2016

compel it to stop pursuing nuclear weapons, and to create incentives for other states to comply with these measures. The UN Security Council first imposed sanctions in resolution 1695 (2006) on the DPRK after the DPRK had carried out a missile launch test in July 2006 and failed to comply with its international obligations under resolutions 825 (1993) and 1540 (2006). This was followed by UNSC resolution 1718 (2006) after the DPRK's first nuclear test in October 2006, which imposed an arms embargo, a ban on trade for goods that could support the DPRK's nuclear and ballistic missile programs and asset freezes and travel bans for entities and persons found to be part of the DPRK's nuclear program. Resolution 1718 also set up a sanctions committee to monitor the imposition of sanctions against North Korea and prohibited the trade of luxury goods. Since 2006, the UN has continuously passed resolutions strengthening and expand its sanctions regime against the DPRK.[11] The current UN sanctions regime includes over a dozen resolutions which mostly were passed following nuclear or ballistic missile tests by the DPRK.[12] Successive resolutions have expanded the sanctions to encompass a comprehensive arms embargo, a freezing of all assets of entities of the North Korean regime or entities and persons linked to its nuclear weapons program, a travel ban for designated individuals or persons acting on behalf of such individuals and extensive restrictions to financial services to the DPRK. The UN has over time also expanded its trade ban on the DPRK to include coal, minerals, crude oil, refined petroleum, natural gas, aviation fuel, textiles, luxury goods, and seafood. Another central aspect of UN sanctions are its provisions regarding the interdiction, transportation, and disposal of the prohibited items mentioned above.

In addition to having transposed and implemented the relevant UN resolutions and their provisions discussed above, the EU has also adopted autonomous sanctions against the DPRK and has designated additional entities and persons found to support North Korea's nuclear and ballistic weapons program. Autonomous restrictions implemented by the EU mostly expand the list of items, goods, and technologies that have been sanctioned by the UN in an effort by the EU to supplement and reinforce the respective UN sanctions. However, none of the EU's autonomous measures encompass areas or sectors that have not been subject to UN restrictions. Nonetheless, the EU has currently listed 60 persons and 9 entities on its DPRK sanctions list autonomously (Council Decision (CFSP) 2016/849 and Council Regulation (EU) 2017/1509),[13] complementing the UN designation of 80 persons and 75 entities.

---

[11] The UN Security Council resolutions laying out sanctions measures against the DPRK are 1874 (2009), 2087 (2012), 2094 (2013), 2270 (2016), 2321 (2016), 2356 (2017), 2371 (2017), 2375 (2017), and 2397 (2017).

[12] The DPRK has conducted 6 nuclear tests and numerous ballistic missile tests, including an Intercontinental Ballistic Missile (ICBM) test in 2017 and a Submarine-launched Ballistic Missile (SLBM) test in 2019.

[13] For the consolidated version, including relevant amendments, of Decision 2016/849, visit data.europa.eu/eli/dec/2016/849/2019-07-18. For Regulation 2017/1509, visit data.europa.eu/eli/reg/2017/1509/2019-07-18

The USA also maintains a number of sanctions against the DPRK in addition to implementing the UN resolutions discussed above. While previously the USA had restricted trade with North Korea under the Trading with the Enemy Act of 1917 (TWEA), the current US sanctions regime began in 2008 with the termination of the authorities under the TWEA and the issuance of E.O. 13466 declaring a national emergency in response to the threat posed by the nuclear proliferation risk stemming from the DPRK. E.O. 13466 essentially continued the restrictions on trade with North Korea as initially granted under the TWEA. However, while the restrictions remained very similar, issuing executive orders grants more flexibility and power to the US president in expanding and adjusting sanctions measures. The USA subsequently imposed an asset freeze on persons and entities involved in the North Korean nuclear program by E.O. 13551 (2010) and further expanded by E.O. 13687 (2015), an arms embargo in line with UN resolutions under E.O. 13570 (2011) and restrictions on the government of North Korea by E.O. 13722 (2016). In September 2017, E.O. 13810 was passed restricting access to the US financial system and freezing assets of entities trading with North Korea. The USA also passed the North Korea Sanctions and Policy Enhancement Act of 2016 which imposes further sanctions on entities involved in the DPRK's weapons of mass destruction program, arms trade, human rights abuses, or other illegal activities, including new sanctions on entities engaged in cybersecurity abuse. North Korea was also included in CAATSA alongside Iran and Russia in 2017, which enhances the US President's authority to impose sanctions on persons violating UN resolutions, restricts financial institutions engagement with third party institutions if they provide financial services to the DPRK, restricts aid and assistance to countries engaged in arms trade with the DPRK, sanctions DPRK transportation and goods and sanctions entities employing North Koran workers. The DPRK was also included again by the USA in its state sponsor of terrorism list in 2017, after having been removed in 2008. The inclusion on this list triggered the same restrictions on North Korea as discussed above with regard to Iran's listing. The development of sanctions against North Korea can be seen in the following diagrams (Figs. 3.4, 3.5 and 3.6).

3.4 Russia

The sanctions currently in place against Russia came in response to its illegal annexation of the Crimean Peninsula in March 2014, its military involvement in Eastern Ukraine, as well as the unprovoked and illegal invasion of Ukraine in February 2022. However, contrary to the Iranian and North Korean cases, the foundation for the international sanctions regime against Russia is not based on UN Security Council resolutions. This is due to the fact that Russia as a permanent member of the Security Council can veto any resolution trying to impose sanctions against Russia and has thus resisted attempts at incurring sanctions for its military intervention in Ukraine.

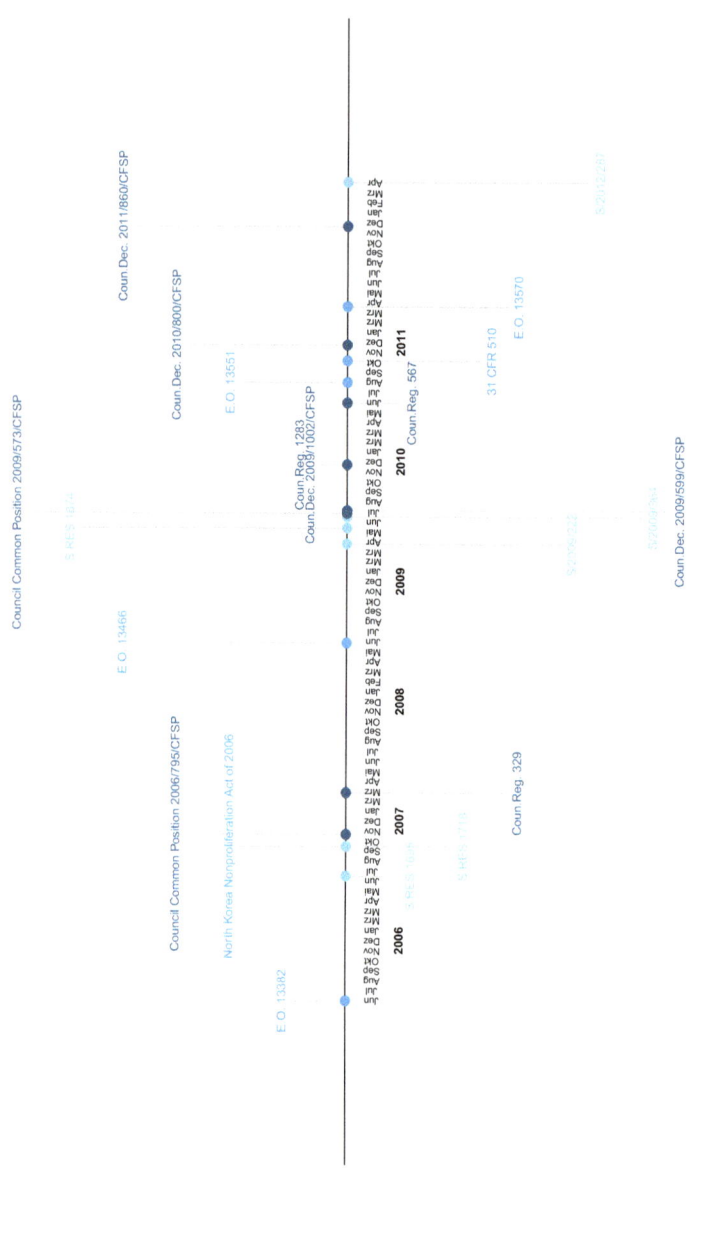

Fig. 3.4 Sanctions against North Korea between 2005 and 2012

3.4 Russia

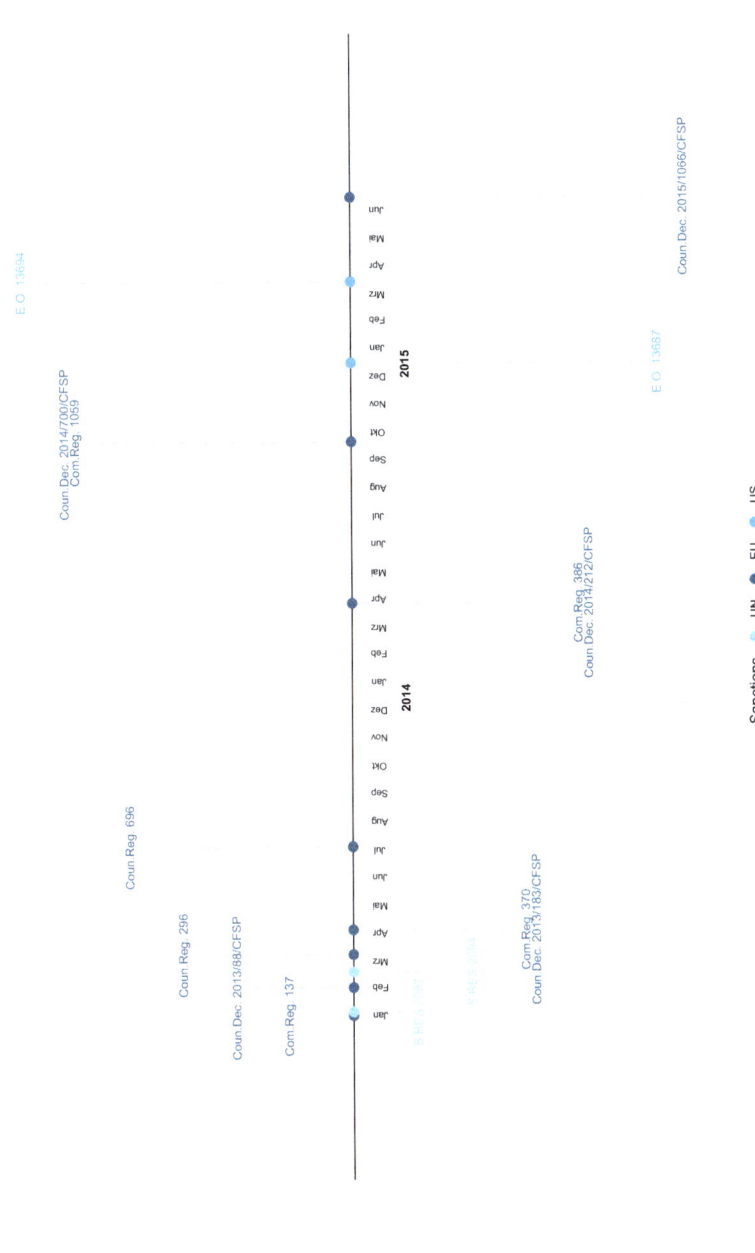

Fig. 3.5 Sanctions against North Korea between 2012 and 2016

28   3 Measures

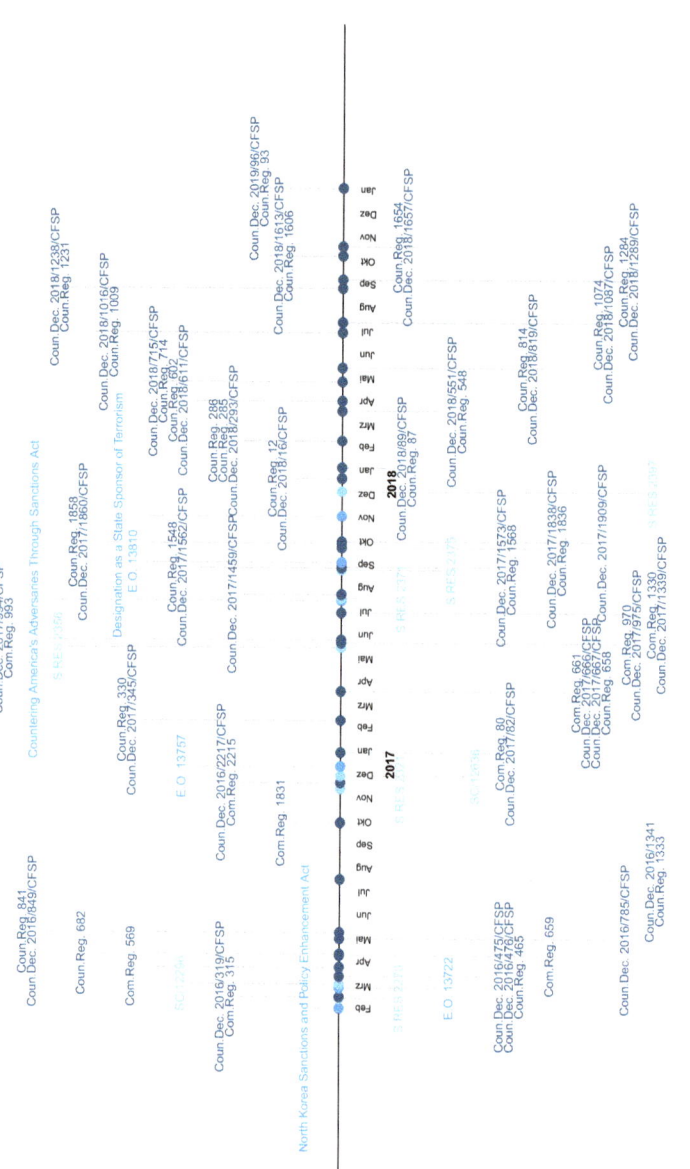

Fig. 3.6 Sanctions against North Korea after 2016

3.4 Russia

Nonetheless, both the EU and the USA have imposed a number of sanctions and restrictive measures against Russia. It is noteworthy that the EU has repeatedly underlined that a lifting of these measures was tied to the full implementation of the Minsk peace agreement of 2015. The USA in contrast has not provided a clear set of steps to be taken by Russia for the US Ukraine/Russia-related sanctions to be lifted. Following the Russian invasion, sanctions imposition and hence the prospect of their lifting are part of the effort to end the Russian invasion and restore Ukrainian sovereignty for both the EU and USA, making at least partial sanctions lifting likely in the case of a Russian retreat (Timofeev, 2022). After the Crim annexation, the EU adopted sanctions measures pertaining to three different areas. First, the EU has imposed sanctions in the form of asset freezes and travel bans on Russian and Ukrainian persons and entities for their involvement in the annexation of Crimea and the destabilization of eastern Ukraine under Council Decision 2014/145/CFSP of March 2014 and its relevant amendments and updates.[14] The EU's specially designated nationals list is continuously updated and included at least 177 individuals and 48 entities before the Russian invasion (the lists now include 1158 individuals and 98 entities). Second, the EU imposed sectoral sanctions on entities operating in the Russian financial, energy, and defense area. These economic sanctions were imposed under Council Decision 2014/512/CFSP of July 2014 and include restrictions on investments, arms, and dual-use items trade and sale of goods and technology used for different oil development projects.[15] The targeted entities included five major state-controlled Russian banks (including Sberbank, VTB, and Gazprombank), three defense firms (United Aircraft Corporation and two Rostec subsidiaries), and three energy companies (Gazpromneft, Rosneft, and Transneft). Finally, the EU also restricted EU trade with the Crimean Peninsula as well as investments in some economic sectors and infrastructure projects under Council Decision 2014/386/CFSP of June 2014.[16] The EU also introduced Council Decision (CFSP) 2018/1544 of 15 October 2018 that allows for the imposition of sanctions on entities and persons for their involvement with and the use of chemical weapons. Subsequently, in January 2019 the EU designated four Russian intelligence officers (GRU) for their role in the poisoning of Sergei Skripal and his daughter.

As with the EU sanctions, the USA imposed sanctions against Russia in response to the conflict in Ukraine. The basis for these restrictions are the E.O.s 13660, 13661, 13662, and 13685 issued in 2014 by former US President Obama. They provide for asset freezes and travel bans on Russian and Ukrainian persons and entities for their involvement in the annexation of Crimea. E.O. 13685 also includes a prohibition for trading of any goods, services, or technology to or from the Crimea region of Ukraine and prohibits new investment in the Crimea region of Ukraine by US persons. They also enable the USA to impose sanctions against members of the Russian government, persons who operate in the Russian arms sector and persons

---

[14] For the consolidated version, visit data.europa.eu/eli/dec/2014/145(1)/2019-09-14.
[15] For the consolidated version, visit data.europa.eu/eli/dec/2014/512/2019-12-21.
[16] For the consolidated version, visit data.europa.eu/eli/dec/2014/386/2019-06-22.

who operate in the Russian financial and energy sectors. The provisions contained in these E.O.s were further extended, amended, and codified in the Titel II of CAATSA—Countering Russian Influence in Europe and Eurasia Act of 2017 (CRIEEA). In general, the measures taken are closely coordinated with the EU and hence the US and EU sanctions regime are very similar, although not identical. Nonetheless, while the EU has imposed sanctions primarily in response to the crisis in Ukraine, the USA has imposed additional sanctions in response to other areas of Russian "malicious" activities. These include sanctions against Russia and Russian persons and entities for human rights violations and corruption issued under the Sergei Magnitsky Act (2012), the Global Magnitsky Act (2016), and E.O. 13818 (2017); malicious activity in cyberspace, including cyberattacks and interference in the 2016 US presidential election, under E.O. 13694 (2015, amended in 2016 by E.O. 13757) and relevant CRIEEA sections, the use of chemical weapons under the Chemical And Biological Weapons Control and Warfare Elimination Act of 1991 (CBW) in response to a US assessment that Russia poisoned Sergei Skripal and his daughter in March 2018 with a nerve agent.[17] Entities and persons listed under either of these measures have their assets frozen, export restrictions apply and are in general prohibited from dealing with US firms and entities. Additionally, the CBW Act triggers restrictions on arms sales, foreign military assistance and foreign financial assistance, halting lending and export of goods or technology listed in the list of controlled items established in the Export Administration Act of 1979. The development of sanctions against Russia can be seen in Fig. 3.7 and 3.8.

---

[17] See the US State Departments press statement announcing that Russia has been determined to be in violation of international law relating to the use of chemical weapons www.state.gov/imposition-of-chemical-and-biological-weapons-control-and-warfare-elimination-act-sanctions-on-russia/

3.4 Russia

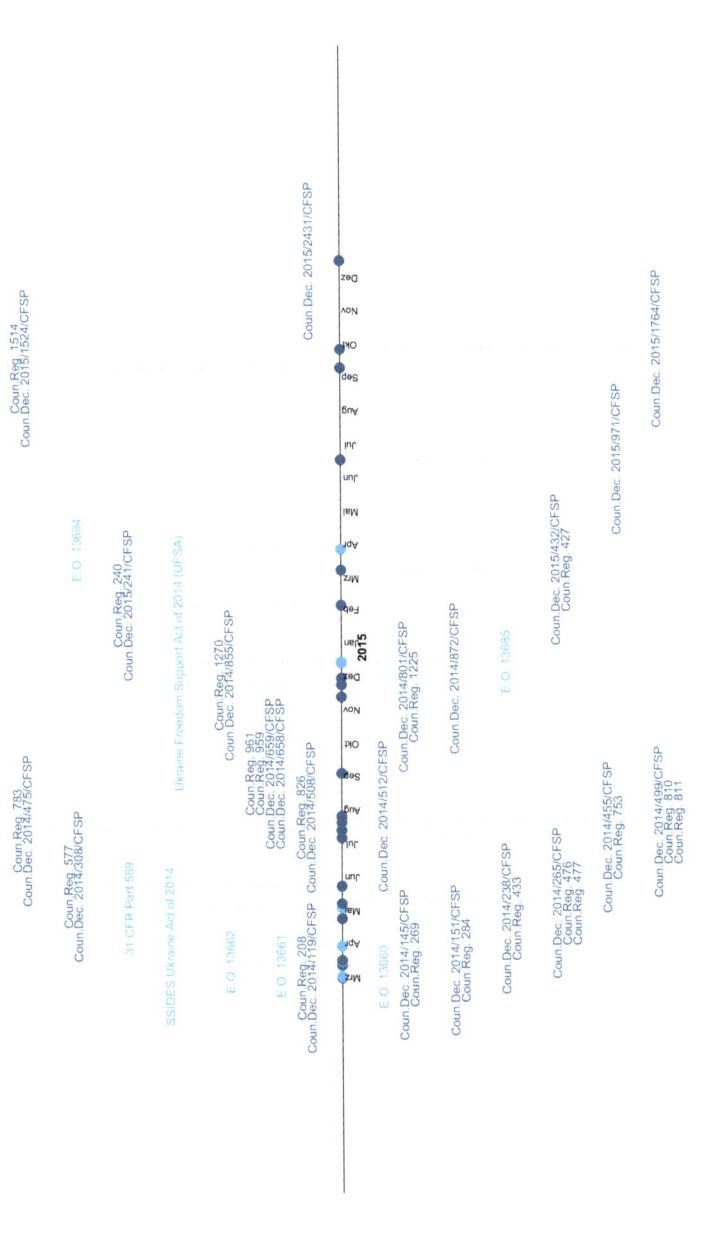

Fig. 3.7 Sanctions against Russia between 2014 and 2016

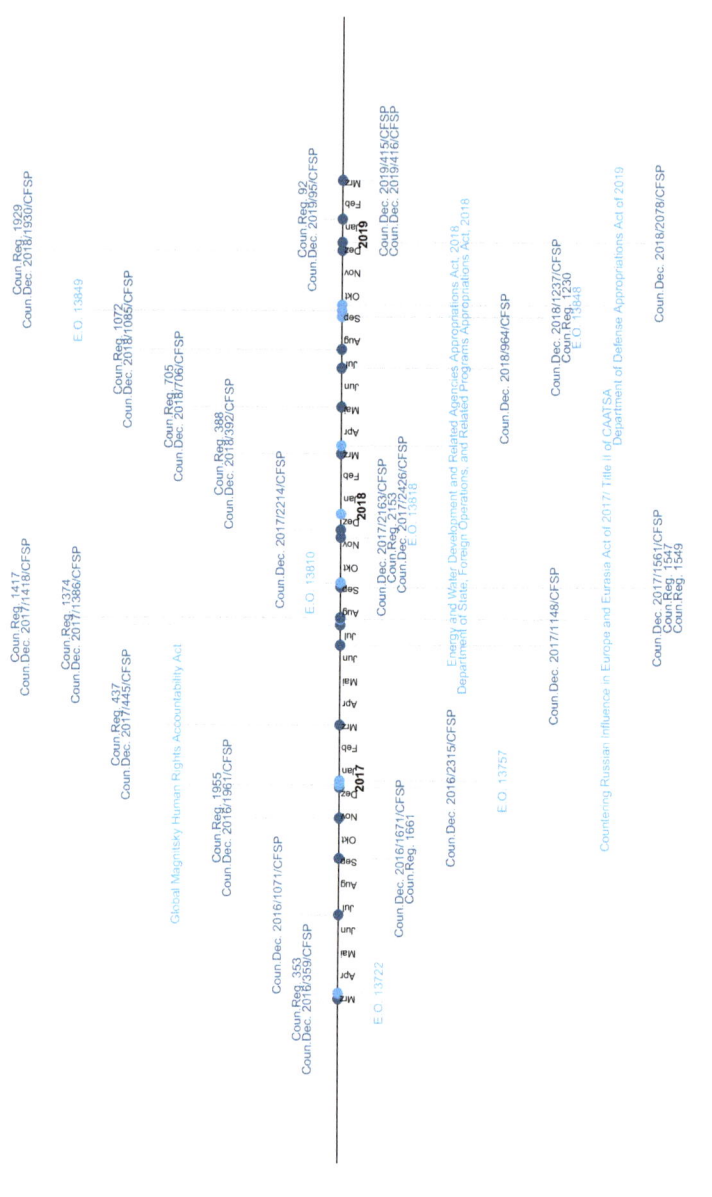

Fig. 3.8 Sanctions against Russia after 2016

Chapter 4
Effects of Sanctions on North Korea, Iran, and Russia

As with both objectives and measures, effects of sanctions can vary greatly in what form they take. Furthermore, in line with how measures can have both intermediate objectives and end-goals, effects can also be categorized according to their immediate impact, which in most cases is economic, financial, or diplomatic, as well as to their ultimate outcome, which is mostly political in nature. As discussed in the previous section on objectives of sanctions, this split in categorization stems from the long standing discussion on the effectiveness of sanctions. With one group of scholars arguing that effectiveness of sanctions has to ultimately be judged based on if they managed to achieve their (political) objectives, while others maintain that sanctions can be viewed as effective if they manage to impose high enough costs to the target state, even if the objectives are not fully achieved[1]. It should be noted though that sanctions which do not lead to a change in behavior of the targeted state can hardly be called effective. As both approaches can provide valuable insights, the section below discusses both the political effects and the economic impact of sanctions on the three targeted countries.

Supplementary Information The online version contains supplementary material available at https://doi.org/10.1007/978-3-031-17397-4_4.

---

[1] It has to be noted, however, that regardless of which approach one prefers, the effect of sanctions is notoriously difficult to disentangle from other developments of the global economy or from geopolitical developments. Most notably for our cases, it is difficult to separate the effect sanctions had from developments in global energy markets, given Russia's and Iran's high reliance on energy exports.

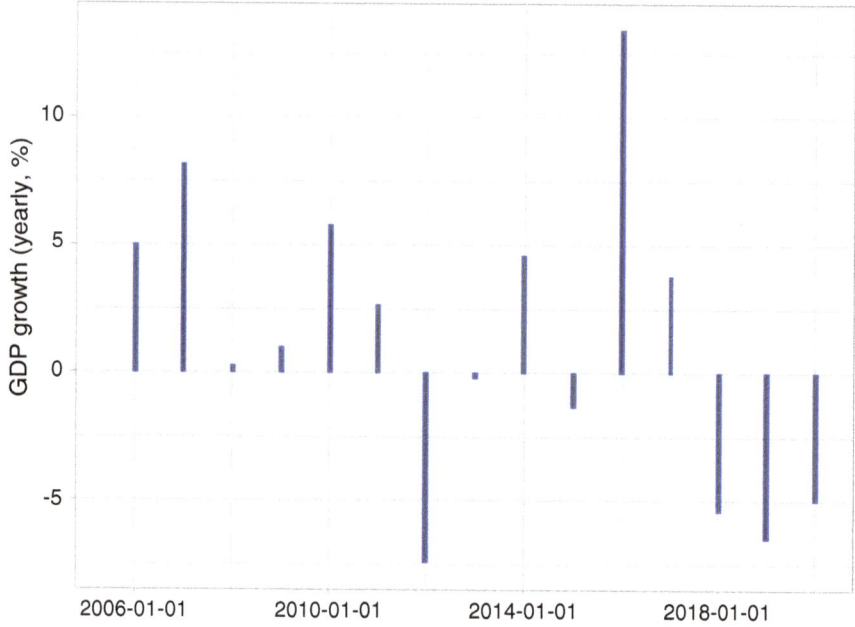

Fig. 4.1 GDP growth in Iran 2006–2020 (World Bank Global Development Indicators, Statista)

4.1 Iran

The impact of sanctions on Iran are the most visible, particularly with regard to achieving a political objective. Most analysts and scholars agree that the international sanctions regime played a major role in bringing Iran to the negotiation table resulting in the JCPOA in 2015 (Katzman, 2020). However, with the USA unilaterally leaving the JCPOA and reintroducing new nuclear-related sanctions in 2018, it has yet to be seen if unilateral sanctions under the "maximum pressure" strategy of the USA will be able to achieve the same intended effect. Furthermore, sanctions that remained in place over Iran's regional activities and its human rights violations seem to not have been able to change Iran's behavior in both regards (see, e.g., Human Rights Watch, 2016).

Nonetheless, sanctions had a strong effect on most macroeconomic indicators during both the multilateral sanctions regime, particularly after their tightening in the 2010–2015 period, and the unilateral sanctions imposed by the USA since 2018 (Figs. 4.1 and 4.2).

Between 2011 and 2015 Iran's GDP fell by around 20% mostly due to reductions in oil exports after the USA and the EU imposed sanctions on trade with Iran's oil sector. Iranian oil sales during that time fell by over one million barrels per day from 2.5 million barrels per day in 2011. The renewed US sanctions imposed since 2018 have had a similar effect with Iran's economy reportedly declining almost 8% from the beginning of 2019 to the beginning of 2020. Crude oil exports from Iran declined

4.1 Iran

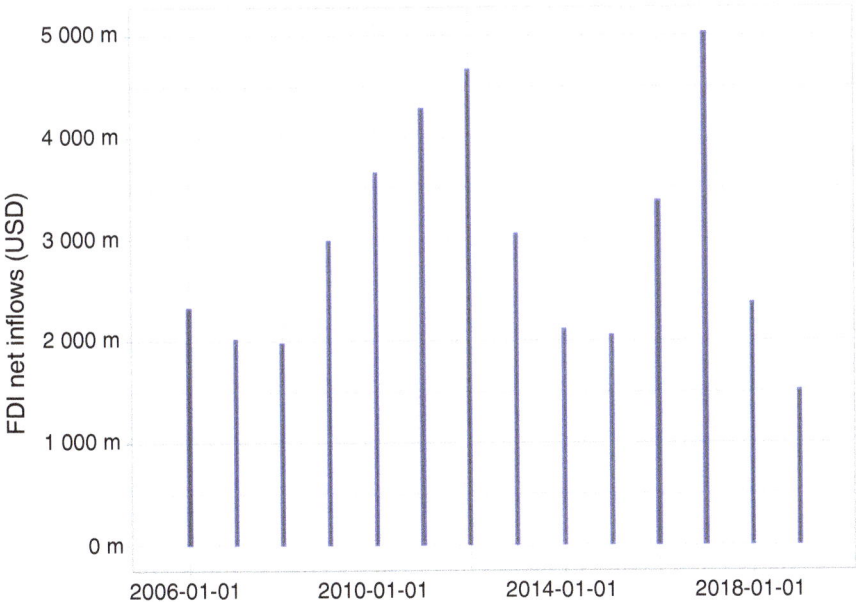

Fig. 4.2 Foreign Direct Investment in Iran 2006–2020 (World Bank Global Development Indicators)

even more strongly than during the 2011–2015 period with Iran having only exported 0.57 million barrels per day in 2019 compared to 2.15 in 2016. This effect is only further exacerbated by the current global pandemic that has a strong negative impact on the Iranian economy (The World Bank, 2020a). Iran has been hit by the pandemic exceptionally hard. Sanctions also had a strong negative impact on foreign direct investment (FDI) in Iran. Particularly during the multilateral sanctions period FDI net inflows more than halved to 2.05 billion in 2015. Similarly, while FDI inflows rebounded during the JCPOA, they reached record lows after the USA reimposed their sanctions resulting in a drop of FDI net inflows from US\$5 billion in 2017 to US\$1.5 billion in 2019. Apart from GDP growth and FDI inflows, the multilateral and the unilateral US sanctions period also seems to overlap with periods of higher unemployment and inflation rates. The official USD–Rial exchange rate, on the other hand, has just continuously increased, even with the Iranian government attempting to artificially control it, from 10,000 rial for US\$1 in 2010 to over 47,000 rial for US\$1 in 2020[2] (Figs. 4.3, 4.4, and 4.5).

---

[2] It has to be noted here that the development of the inofficial "open market based" exchange rate has undergone an even steeper development, with the official rate valuing the rial far above market rates.

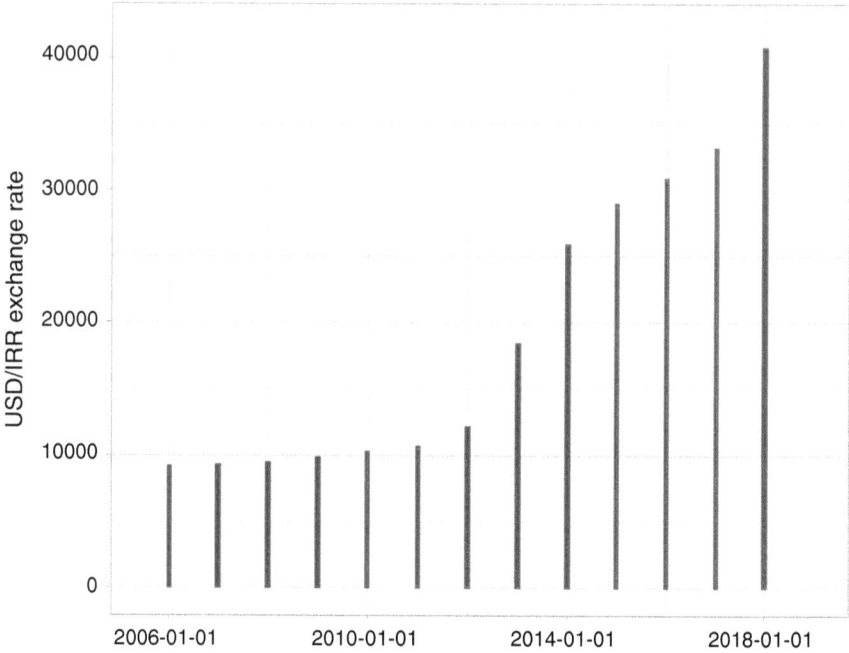

Fig. 4.3 Change in USD/IRR exchange rate 2006–2020 (World Bank Global Development Indicators)

4.2 North Korea

Assessing the effect of sanctions is, as noted earlier, difficult, even more so with regard to North Korea since economic data is mostly unavailable with the North Korean regime not providing access to official statistics on economic performance. Furthermore, due to the global sanctions regime in place, North Korea has substituted much of its trade relationship with relying on illicit channels for acquiring goods. Nonetheless, this section provides an attempt at identifying the effect sanctions have had on North Korea. Sanctions have not been able to deter North Korea to continue its nuclear weapons program as exemplified by an increasing number of nuclear and ballistic missile tests since Kim Jong-un's ascension to power. Most likely due to the impact of UN and US sanctions the North Korean leadership has announced a moratorium on nuclear and ICBM tests in 2018. However, North Korea's reliance on illicit channels to acquire finances, goods, and technology also highlights that the sanctions are impacting the North Korean economy as well as potentially hindering its nuclear weapons program. Nonetheless, it is unlikely that this will lead to a behavioral change on part of North Korea and neither is it clear that the sanctions will be able to destabilize the regime to a degree that could lead to regime change (Mangott & Senn, 2017). So far, the North Korean regime has provided to be very resilient to the sanctions pressure. With regard to

4.2 North Korea

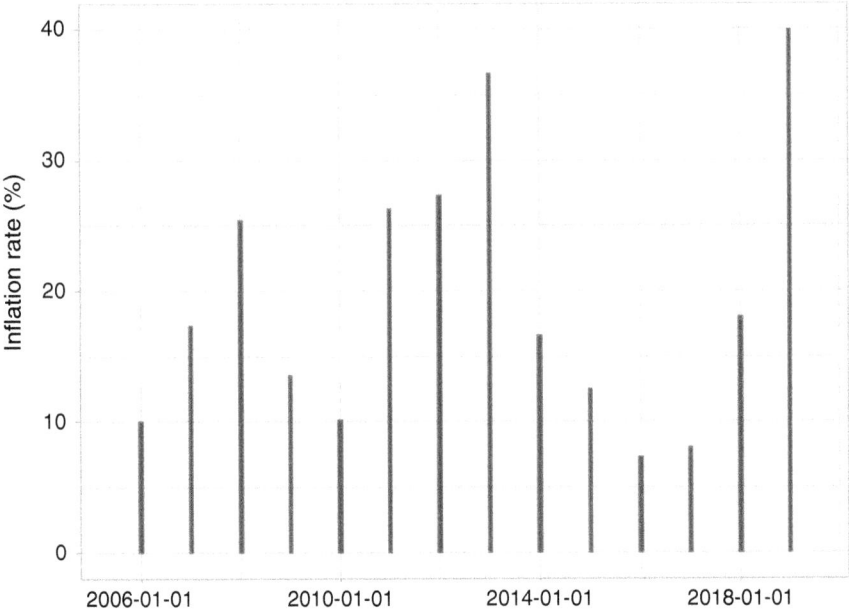

Fig. 4.4 Unemployment in Iran 2006–2020 (World Bank Global Development Indicators)

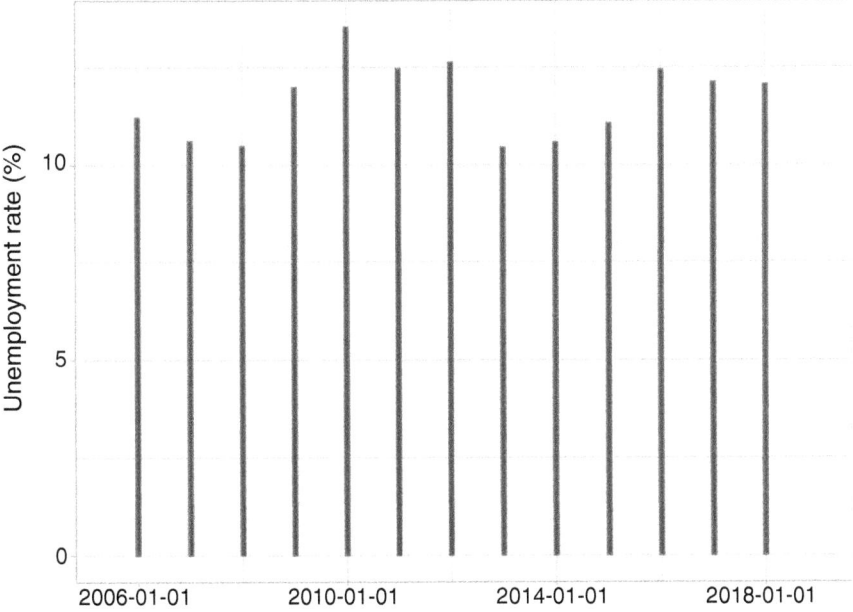

Fig. 4.5 Inflation in Iran 2006–2020

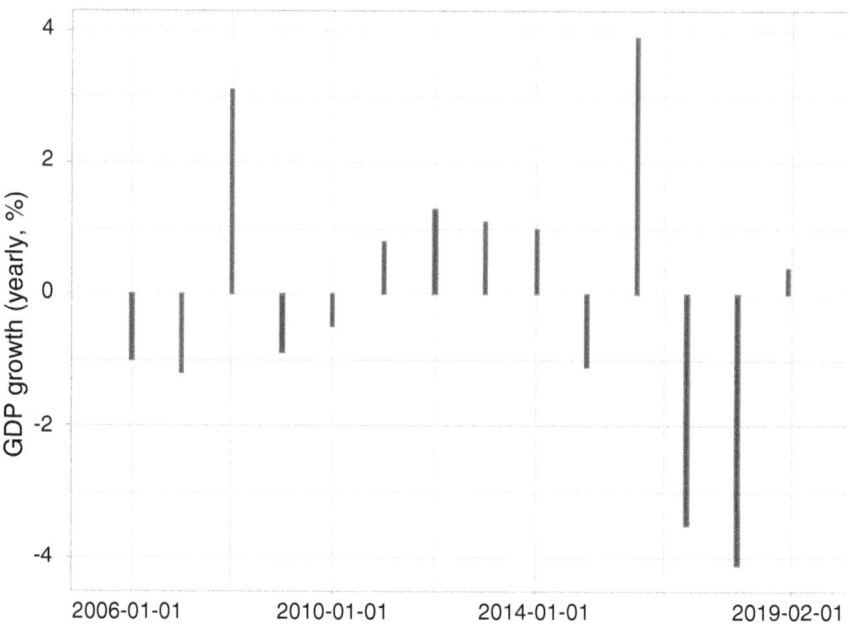

Fig. 4.6 GDP growth in North Korea 2006–2019 (Bank of Korea Economics Statistics System)

economic effects there have been some notable developments in the country's economy and trade relations, particularly in response to the tightening of the sanctions regime in 2016. Estimates by the Bank of Korea suggest that sanctions affected North Korea's GDP growth, with negative GDP growth rates after sanctions were introduced in 2006, 2009, and 2016. This economic downturn continues with GDP growth rates of −3.5% in 2017, −4.1% in 2018, and 0.4% in 2019 which at least in part can be attributed to the major extensions of sanctions starting in 2016 (Fig. 4.6). The tightening of sanctions against North Korea also coincides with a strong downturn in inflows of FDI with very low or negative net inflows since 2017 (Fig. 4.7). Koen and Beom (2020) further argue that the economic sanctions have reduced foreign currency earnings, resulted in an altered domestic industrial structure, and affected foreign trade. Specifically, with trade, the sanctions had a noticeable effect. While Japan and South Korea stopped all trading with North Korea in 2006 and 2016, respectively, China accounted for 95.8% of all of North Korea's trade (compared to 50% in 2005) (Koen & Beom, 2020, p. 25). Furthermore, after the tightening of sanctions in 2016, exports of the newly sanctioned goods, that accounted for a considerable part of total exports, fell drastically, resulting in a reduction of over 60% of total trade value (Figs. 4.8 and 4.9).[3] Arguably however, most of the impact of sanctions the ruling elite has been able to avoid (see, e.g.,

---

[3] All estimates for North Korea do not include illicit trade or other illicit activity that could contribute positively to these numbers. This means that the point estimates produced by the Bank

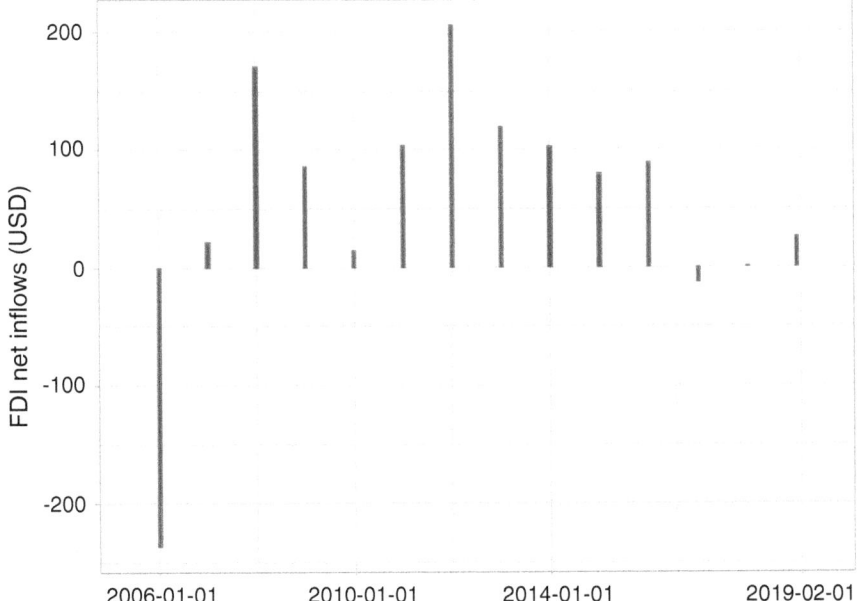

Fig. 4.7 Foreign Direct Investment in North Korea 2006–2019 (UNCTAD

Wong et al., 2020) and most of the costs have affected already marginalized groups in North Korea (see, e.g., Korea Peace Now, 2019). This unequal impact of sanctions is also underlined by Lee (2018) who shows that sanctions result in production shifts toward the capital city, trade hubs close to the Chinese border, and manufacturing cities, hence, increasing regional inequalities.

4.3 Russia

As already touched upon in the sections on objectives and measures, sanctions imposed against Russia over the conflict with Ukraine are mostly concerned with resolving the situation in Eastern Ukraine, reversing the annexation of Crimea and of course ending the Russian invasion. At the center, at least for the EU, sanctions were imposed to push Russia to respect the measures agreed on in the Minsk II peace plan in 2015. In this regard the effect of sanctions has been relatively limited. While there was some progress, including some prisoner swaps (Associated Press, 2020), violations of the agreement continued regardless, ultimately culminating in full-scale Russian invasion. In view of the conflict in Eastern Ukraine having continued (and

---

of Korea and other institutions underestimate the real volume of North Korean exports and accordingly the absolute value of revenues generated through them.

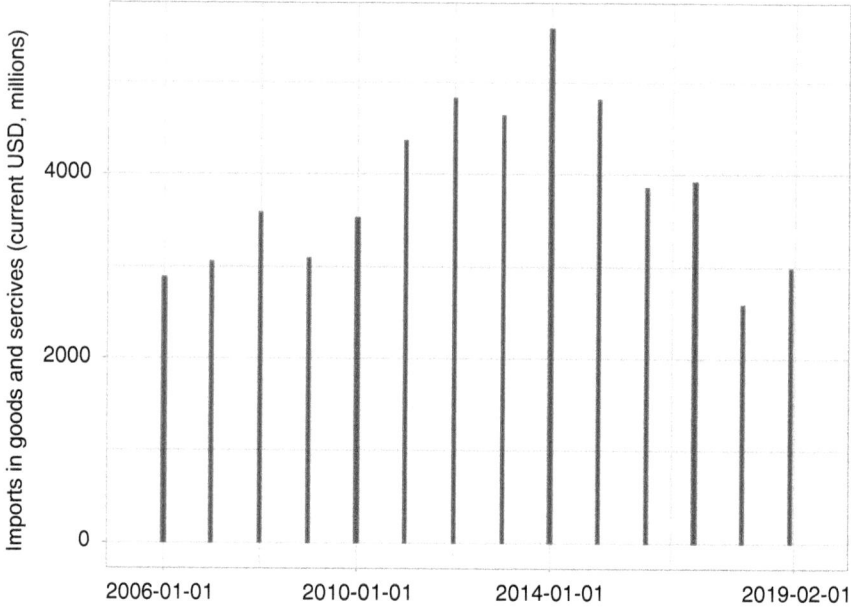

Fig. 4.8 North Korean Exports 2006–2019 (UNCTAD)

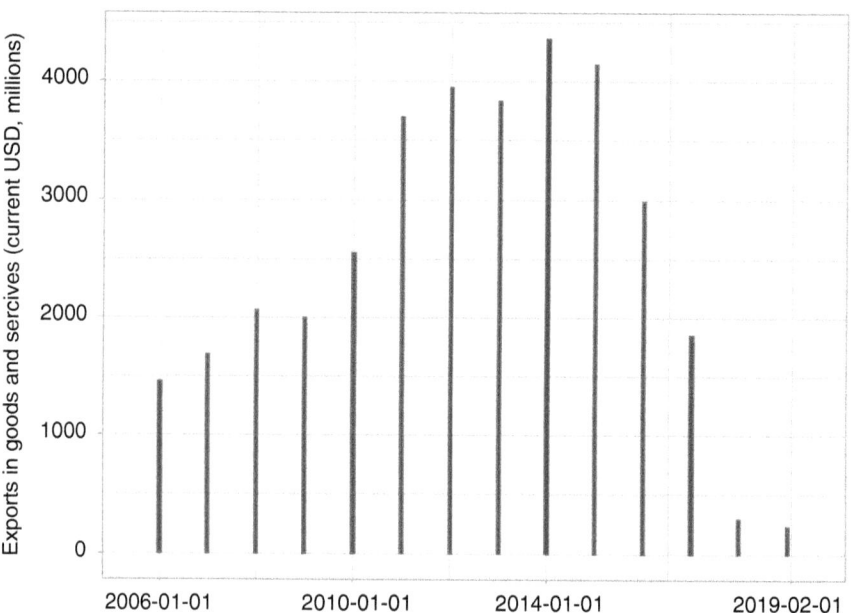

Fig. 4.9 North Korean Imports 2006–2019 (UNCTAD)

finally escalating), including deadly clashes, Russia having providing ammunition, weaponry and fighters, and the situation in Crimea not having changed, sanctions have to be judged as not having been able to achieve the behavioral effect they were intended to have.

While it had been argued that the sanctions, or the threat of more severe measures, were able to help avoid a further escalation of the conflict and constrained Russian actions (Gould-Davies, 2018; Korhonen, 2019), this analysis has now proven to be incorrect. A possible explanation is that since counterfactual analyses, like the ones done by Gould-Davies (2018) and Korhonen (2019), have to rely heavily on strong assumptions about trajectories in national and global economic development, the de-escalatory potential of the sanctions has been put into question. Contrasting arguments highlighted Russia's interest in a limited conflict in order to retain stronger influence in Ukraine. Hence, Russia never had an interest in further escalating the conflict even in the absence of sanctions, which however was, as we now know, blatantly untrue. Nonetheless, the measures imposed by the EU and the USA continue to affect the Russian economy. The International Monetary Fund (2019) Staff Report on the Russian Federation, for example, estimated that the economic sanctions imposed against Russia reduced the GDP growth rate by around 0.2% per year between 2014 and 2018 and has hence contributed—albeit marginally—to the economy's growth slowdown in recent years (Fig. 4.10). However, most of the Russian economy's slowdown can be attributed to the decline in

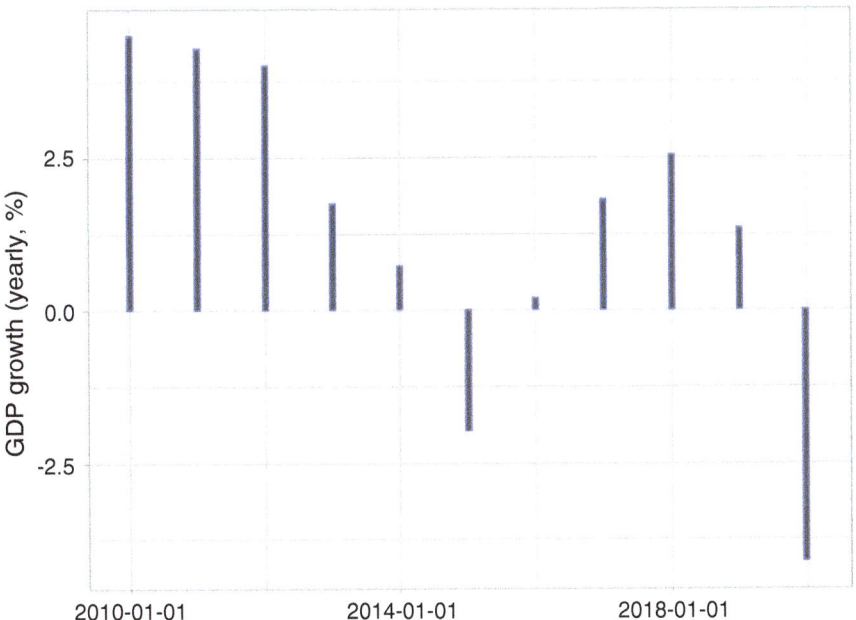

Fig. 4.10 GDP growth in Russia 2010–2020 (World Bank Global Development Indicators, Statista)

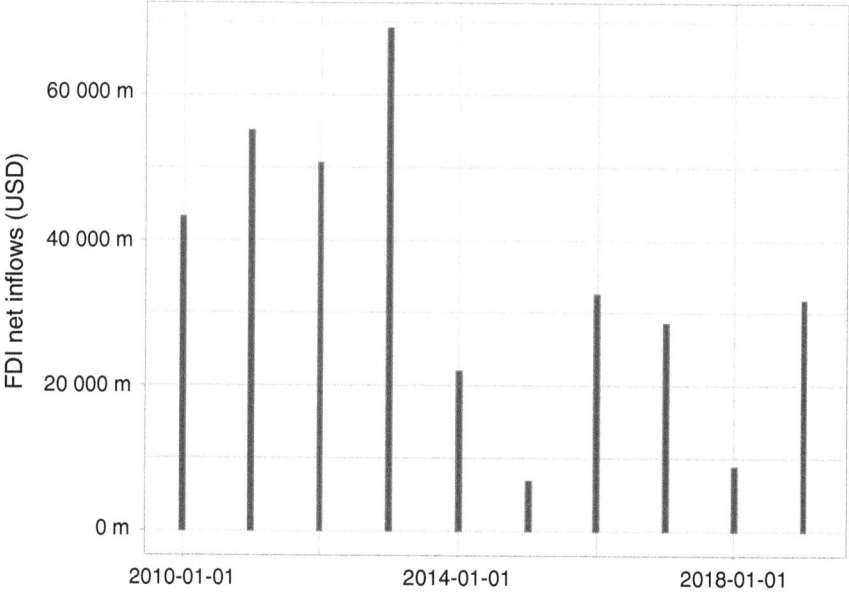

Fig. 4.11 Foreign Direct Investment in Russia 2010–2020 (World Bank Global Development Indicators, Statista)

global oil prices. Nonetheless, the impact of sanctions should not only be judged by its effect slowing down the Russian economy's growth rate.[4] More importantly, it is informative to look at how sanctions have affected the targeted sectors. In general, Russian companies still rely heavily on foreign investment as well as technologies and skills from foreign companies, most notably international oil companies (Gould-Davies, 2018, p. 11). The impact sanctions had in this regard can be seen when looking at the developments of foreign direct investment (FDI) in Russia, with net inflows more than halving from $69.219 billion in 2013 to $31.783 billion in 2019 (The World Bank, 2020b) (Fig. 4.11). Although Russia has sought to substitute this downturn in FDI by increasingly seeking investments from Chinese companies, as can be seen in Fig. 4.11, this has not yet resulted in a return to pre-sanctions FDI values. In addition, a number of Western companies have shelved development projects with Russian energy companies. Exxon, for example, cited Western sanctions for its decision to withdraw from a $500 billion investment into an exploration partnership with Rosneft (Scheyder & Soldatkin, 2018). Furthermore, many economists argue that while Russia has made some important economic adjustments to

---

[4] See also Kholodilin and Netšunajev (2019) who provide an alternative estimation method of the impact sanctions had. They argue that according to their estimation sanctions had a negligible impact on the Russian economy's growth. In contrast to their study, Barseghyan (2019, p. 20) finds that sanctions and the Russian counter-sanctions "induced decreases in real GDP per capita, FDI net inflows."

4.3 Russia

ward off bigger macroeconomic effects, the impact of sanctions will be most notable in the mid- to long-term as they curtail investments in major projects, particularly with regard to shale and offshore gas exploitation (Foy, 2020). However, in the short term the sanctions coincided with a spike in inflation and unemployment rates (Figs. 4.12 and 4.13). Given that both rates quickly returned to their pre-sanctions levels it is hard to attribute this development to the effect of sanctions. This seems to be in line with the argument that the imposed sanctions alone have not been sufficient to strongly affect the Russian economy (see for example the development of Russian imports and exports in Figs. 4.14 and 4.15). Nonetheless, the sanctions period does overlap with a large increase in the USD-RUB exchange rate, although again, the most important factor in this development are the falling oil prices which heavily affected the Russian economy (Fig. 4.16). However, the sanctions imposed also impact the advanced technology Russia requires to develop more difficult to access energy reserves. According to Korhonen et al. (2018) the value of Russian imports of oil technology products fell by around 40% between 2014 and 2016, with Russia appearing to not being able to easily find alternative exporters of these technologies. However, these trends could also be impacted by the general decline in oil prices during that period. A final impact sanctions had on the Russian economy is through its targeting of specific individuals and companies connected to the situation in Eastern Ukraine and Crimea. Ahn and Ludema (2019) investigate how companies that were directly listed on US or EU sanctions lists performed compared

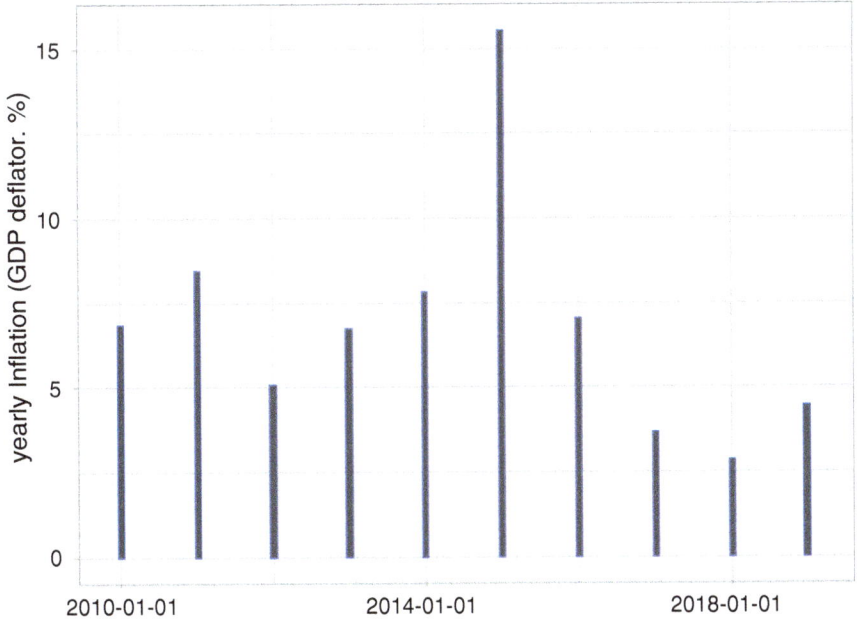

Fig. 4.12 Inflation in Russia 2010–2020 (World Bank Global Development Indicators)

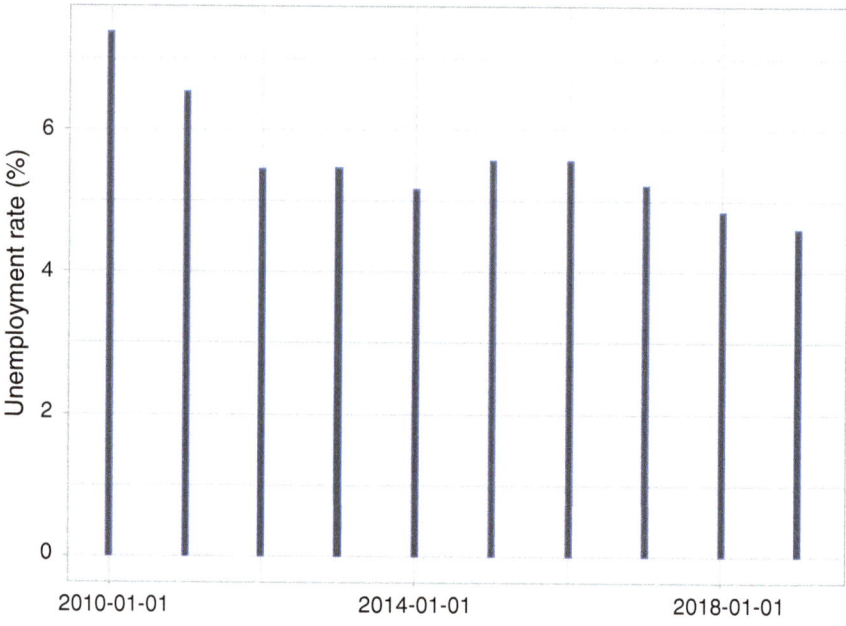

Fig. 4.13 Unemployment in Russia 2010–2020 (World Bank Global Development Indicators)

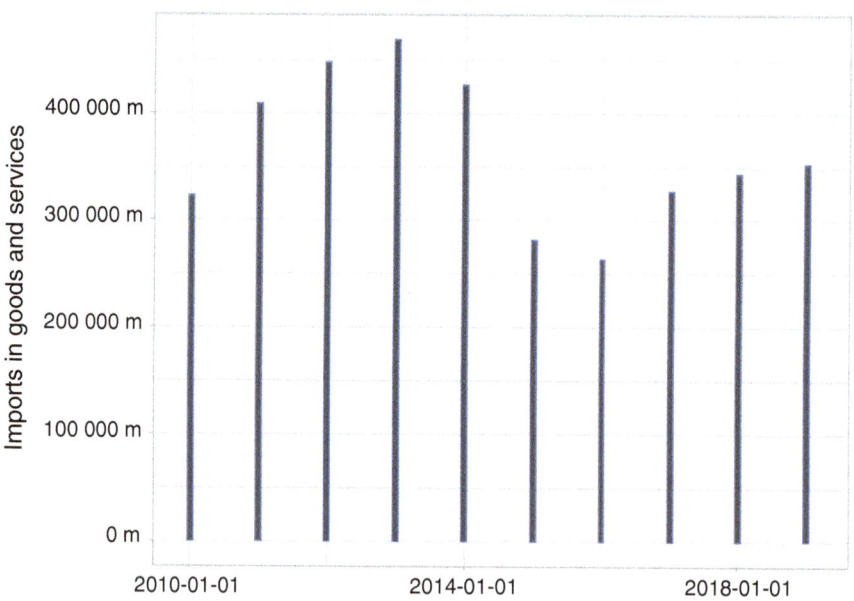

Fig. 4.14 Russian Imports 2010–2020 (World Bank Global Development Indicators)

4.3 Russia

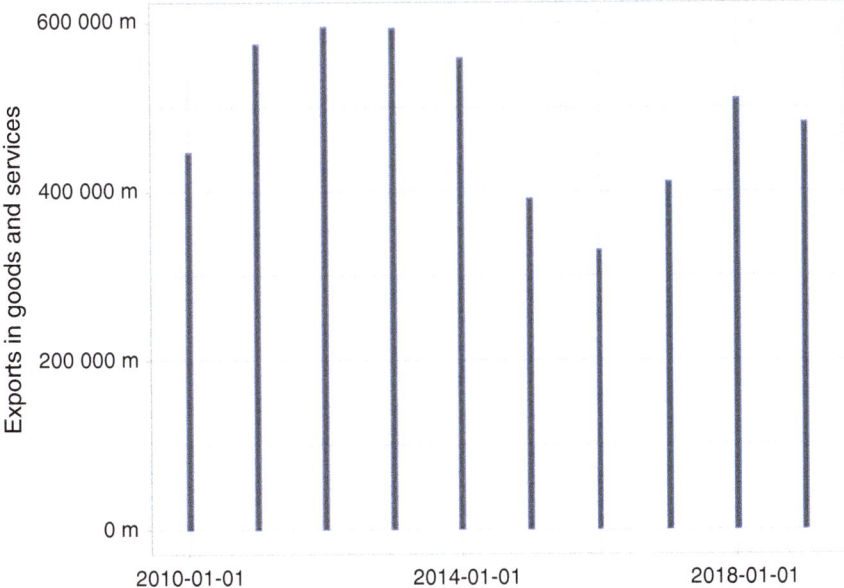

Fig. 4.15 Russian Exports 2010–2020 (World Bank Development Indicators)

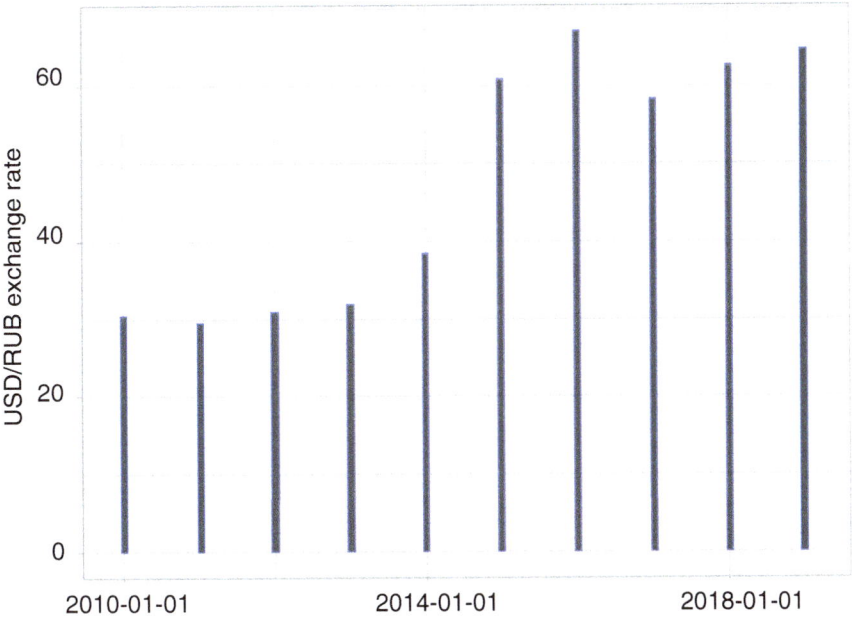

Fig. 4.16 Change in USD/RUB exchange rate 2010–2020 (World Bank Global Development Indicators)

to their non-sanctioned counterparts. They find that sanctioned firms had "significant losses in operating revenue, asset values, and employees" (Ahn & Ludema, 2019, p. 1).

As shown in this section, assessing the effect of sanctions, both in political and economic terms, is not a straightforward exercise because of global economic and geopolitical developments. Another factor, making it more difficult to assess the impact of sanctions is that countries targeted by them often attempt to limit their effect through countermeasures. These countermeasures will be discussed in more detail in the following section.

Chapter 5
Countermeasures

The following section will discuss measures adopted by the three targeted countries to mitigate the effects the sanctions have on their economies. These measures include a variety of actions, from trying to evade sanctions by relying on illicit activities to imposing countersanctions against sender countries. The countermeasures adopted by Russia, Iran, and North Korea are not only a reflection of the sanctions imposed upon them, but also highlight the different positions these three countries occupy in the global economy. This section also further illustrates how imposing sanctions is not without costs to the sender countries.

5.1 Iran

With Iran being the target of sanctions for over four decades, the Iranian regime had ample time to find and test avenues to adjust to them. However, this experience has not necessarily led Iran to be able to avoid the negative impact of sanctions on its economy. Given Iran's strong reliance on oil exports, the options for short-term modifications to address the negative impacts of trade restrictions imposed by the sanctions regime are limited. Nonetheless, Iran has taken a number of steps in response to the sanctions instituted against the country. One of Iran's central strategies that it has pursued for a long time is to further diversify its economy in an attempt to reduce its reliance on oil exports for revenue generation. This long-term strategy has already led to Iran's economy being more diverse than other oil exporting countries, with the agriculture, service provision, manufacturing, and financial sectors becoming important economic pillars (The World Bank, 2020a).

Supplementary Information The online version contains supplementary material available at https://doi.org/10.1007/978-3-031-17397-4_5.

However, growth in these non-oil sectors has been slow and domestic production has not been able to develop at a pace to offset losses in oil exports. Additionally, Iran has sought to accelerate privatization of some of its state-run companies in order to generate extra revenue for the government and narrow its budget deficit (Bozorgmehr & England, 2020). Iran has also sought to adjust its trading partners, mostly by increasing trade with China but neighboring countries also becoming increasingly important after the reimposition of US sanctions and the ending of sanction waivers in 2019. In addition, while the remaining signatories of the JCPOA continue to oppose the US decision to leave the agreement, they are wary of the impact US secondary sanctions could have on their businesses engaging with Iran. In order to alleviate some of those concerns the EU introduced the Instrument in Support of Trade Exchanges (INSTEX) to alleviate some of those concerns and facilitate trade with Iran while avoiding US sanctions. However, the mechanism has so far failed to provide much benefit to facilitating trade between the EU and Iran (Brzozowski, 2020).

Iran also has a long track-record of adopting a number of tactics to evade sanctions. Tactics that Iran employed during the multilateral sanctions period will also likely be employed after the reimposition of unilateral US sanctions. Most of these tactics focus on "obfuscating the origin, destination, and recipient of oil shipments" and while Iran is not unique in this regard (see the section below), Iran has become increasingly proficient in applying various tools like ship-to-ship transfers or using false flags in attempts to evade sanctions (U.S. Department of the Treasury, 2020, p. 33). In addition to continuing oil exports despite sanctions, Iran used these tactics and its networks, until at least 2015, in order to procure items and goods that are prohibited under nuclear proliferation and ballistic missile sanctions (UN Panel of Experts, 2015). A central measure taken by Iran in this regard was to build financial and business structures, including shell companies, to facilitate and finance these procurements. The aim is, similar to Iran's deceptive shipping tactics, to hide who is behind the purchase [see Fig. 5.1 above for an illustrative case reported by the UN Panel of Experts (2015)].

5.2 North Korea

North Korea's strategy to adapt to sanction measures has mostly focused on efforts to develop avenues to bypass the sanctions imposed on the country through illicit means. Furthermore, while North Korea's economy has always been much more isolated from the global economy, it still is strongly dependent on revenue generated by exporting textiles and coal as well as on importing petroleum. One of the central strategies employed by North Korea is focused on deceptive tactics to hide the origin or destination of ships engaged in illicit trade with North Korea. These tactics have enabled North Korea to continue to export, mostly coal and sand, and import, mostly petroleum, goods at levels far above the permissible amount under UN Security Council resolutions (UN Panel of Experts, 2020). The main mechanisms deployed

5.2 North Korea 49

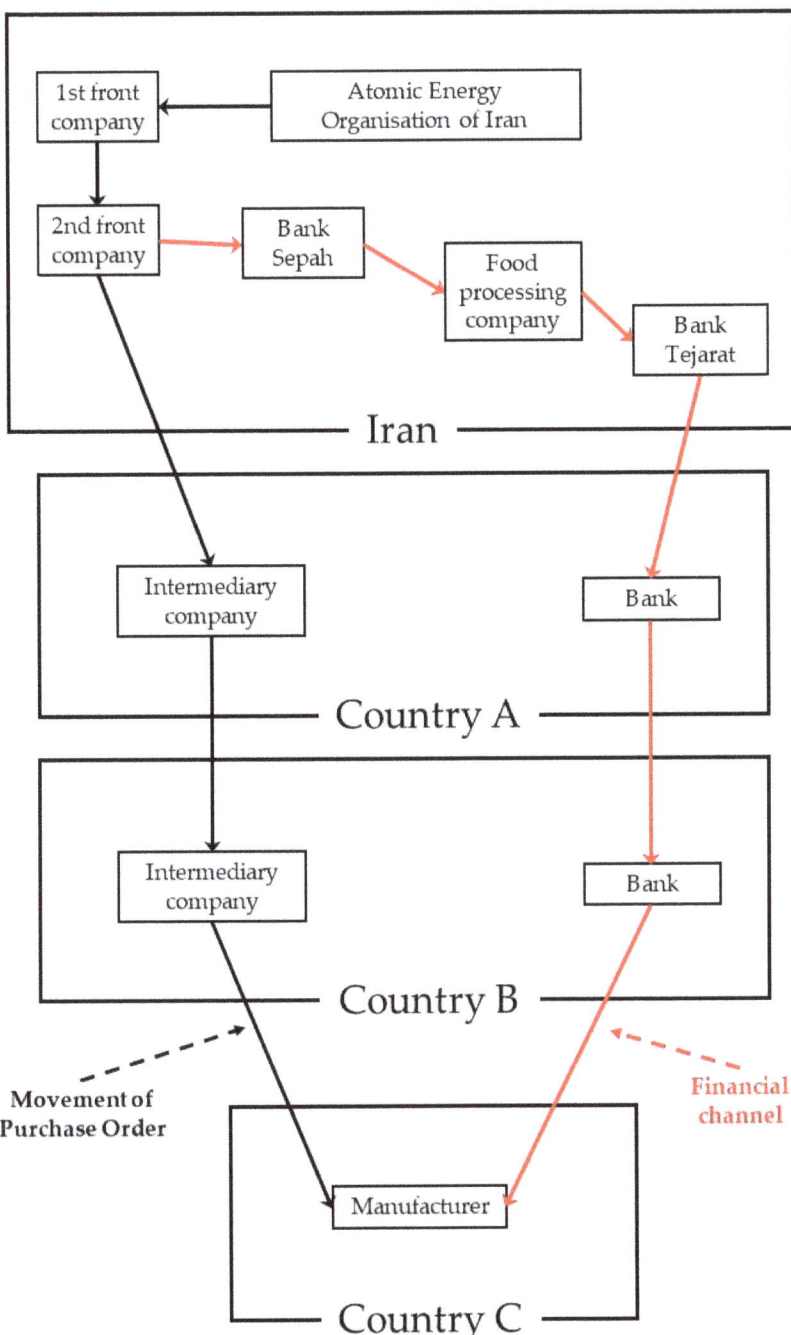

Fig. 5.1 Illustrative case of Iranian procurement mechanism to obfuscate links to sanctioned entities (Atomic Energy Organisation of Iran and Bank Sepah) (Reproduced from UN Panel of Exports 2015 Final Report)

by North Korea include obscuring vessels identity by altering their International Maritime Organization (IMO) number both physically and digitally, falsifying shipping documents, ship-to-ship transfers, using false flags or frequently changing their flags, and hiding their ownership through multi-level business and management structures often including shell companies (Fig. 5.2) (U.S. Department of the Treasury, 2020, pp. 2–3). In addition, the amount of direct deliveries to North Korea's major port in Nampo, both foreign-flagged and DPRK flagged, in violation of UN resolutions has increased significantly and has resulted in North Korea importing between three to eight times the amount of refined petroleum products allowed under UNSC resolutions (UN Panel of Experts, 2020).

North Korea also continues to illegally import luxury goods in an attempt to alleviate the negative effect of sanctions to North Korean elites. This includes luxury goods such as luxury vehicles, watches, and alcohol, highlighting the North Korean illicit networks and supply chains ability to obtain those goods despite the UN ban (Wong et al., 2020). North Korea also generates revenues by illegally selling fishing permits in violation of UNSC resolutions which generated an estimated US$120 million in 2018 (UN Panel of Experts, 2020, p. 43). The country also continues to operate an extensive network to illicitly procure ballistic missile-related technology and materials. A particularly important role in those tactics is played by North Korean diplomats and officials posted overseas (UN Panel of Experts, 2013, p. 25). Using complex business structures, shell companies and North Korean officials to avoid sanctions is not only used for trade and procurement but also to continue to access the international financial system. In this regard, North Korea has also put an emphasis on using illicit cyber-activities to generate revenues. The UN Panel of Experts (2020) assesses that North Korean cyber actors are growing increasingly sophisticated and are engaged in a wide range of activities. Most of the activities are aimed at the international financial sector. Tactics employed by North Korea include financial theft, money laundering, ransomware attacks, cryptojacking, and maintaining cryptocurrency trading platforms (UN Panel of Experts, 2019, pp. 26–30). Finally, as already touched upon in a previous section, North Korea has sought to adjust its legal trade by increasing exports, mostly to China, of commodities not affected by the UN restrictions. With the tightening of sanctions key export products like mineral products, textiles, and seafood were also affected by import restrictions. While exports in these products fell substantially, North Korea sought to substitute those exports with exports of watch parts, feathers, hair and wigs, and medical devices (Koen & Beom, 2020, p. 25). However, so far these alternatives have not been able to make up for the worsening of North Korea's trade deficit.

5.2 North Korea

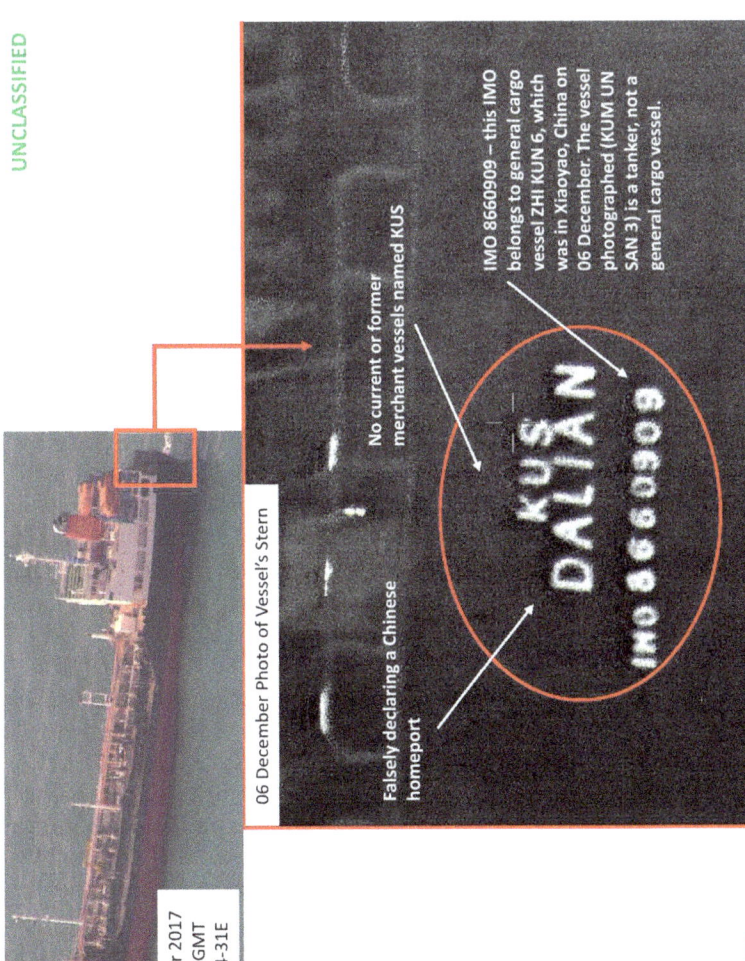

Fig. 5.2 Example of deceptive shipping practices (Reproduced from US Departments of State and Treasury, and US Coast Guard https://home.treasury.gov/policy-issues/financial-sanctions/sanctions-programs-and-country-information/north-korea-sanctions/north-korean-vessels)

5.3 Russia

In contrast to both Iran and North Korea, Russia occupies a much more central role in international relations and the global economy and can hence rely on a bigger arsenal of options in confronting US and EU sanctions. Following their invasion of Ukraine and the subsequent comprehensive international sanctions regime however, Russia has found itself more isolated. Russian countermeasures to EU and US sanctions focused on three elements: (1) countersanctions in the form of an embargo of agriculture and food products and entry bans on Western politicians, (2) reducing reliance on agricultural imports by increasing its own output capacity, and (3) increasing trade with alternative trade partners, mostly countries of the Eurasian Economic Union as well as China. Furthermore, elements two and three are closely related to the design of the countersanctions and are all part of Russia's considerations in deciding what measures to apply in response to Western sanctions (Hedberg, 2018; Pospieszna et al., 2020). Russian countermeasures were first imposed in March 2014 targeting US and Canadian officials and extended in August 2014 to include an import embargo on a broad range of agricultural products from countries that had imposed sanctions against Russia over the conflict in Eastern Ukraine and Crimea (Crozet & Hinz, 2020, pp. 105–6). Following the tightening of sanctions by the EU, in May 2015 Russia also issued an entry ban against 89 EU politicians and officials (Crozet & Hinz, 2020, p. 105). While it was unsurprising that Russia would implement some countermeasures and the measures against Western individuals were quickly acknowledged as a retaliatory measure, the imposition of the agri-food import ban came as a surprise for many, given Russia's high reliance on agri-food imports from Western countries. The embargoed products, including fruit, vegetables, meat, fish, milk and dairy products, account for more than 50% of agri-food imports to Russia and are valued at almost US$10 billion (European Parliament, 2017, p. 16). Given the close trade ties between them, the import ban had a strong effect on both EU and Russian trade in this sector (Fig. 5.3).[1] However, the Russian countersanctions seem to have been carefully crafted as they have affected the trade with countries that Russia perceives as hostile to Russian foreign policy (e.g., Poland, the Baltic states, Sweden, Denmark, and Norway) or as geostrategic rivals (e.g., USA) more negatively than, for example, countries that Russia views as (potential) important strategic partners (e.g., France, Germany, and Italy) (Hedberg, 2018). Furthermore, the Russian countersanctions were carefully crafted not only to retaliate against sanctioning countries, but also to further long-term domestic political and economic goals. These goals include reducing external

---

[1] See, e.g., the figure on Structure of EU Agri-food trade with Russia (2009–2019) taken from the European Commission (2020, 2) Trade Statistics Factsheet.

5.3 Russia

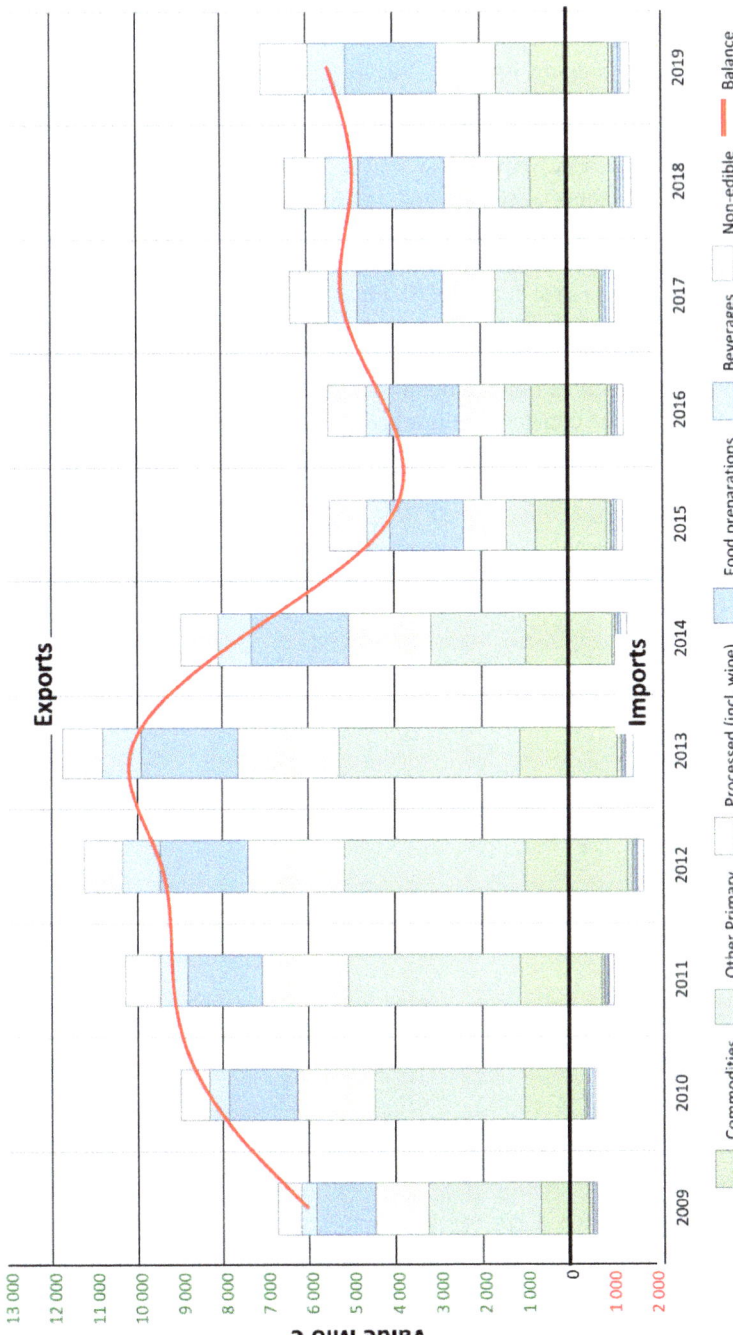

Fig. 5.3 Structure of EU Agri-food trade with Russia 2009–2019 (Reproduced from European Commission Trade Statistical Factsheet, https://ec.europa.eu/info/sites/info/files/food-farming-fisheries/farming/documents/agrifood-russia_en.pdf)

food dependencies, diversifying its trade partnerships, bolstering diplomatic and economic ties to strategically important countries in Asia and South America, and increasing public political support (Hedberg, 2018; Korhonen, 2019; Pospieszna et al., 2020). While judging Russia's "success" in regard to these goals is still difficult given the goals long-term dimension, a preliminary assessment indicates that some progress has been made. As discussed above, countersanctions have affected EU member state exports (to varying degrees). In addition, domestic Russian agricultural output also increased and Russia was able to deepen its trade ties with countries part of the Eurasian Economic Union, Commonwealth of Independent States (CIS) countries, Brazil, Paraguay, and China (see, e.g., European Parliament, 2017; Pospieszna et al., 2020). Finally, as some analysts had suggested, a rally around the flag effect by the Russian population in response to the sanctions and countersanctions seems to have materialized, as approval ratings for Russian president Vladimir Putin and public opinion polls on the topic of countersanctions seem to indicate that the countersanctions had the intended positive effect (see, e.g., Ashford, 2016). However, we still lack conclusive scientific evidence linking these two factors.

Chapter 6
Recent Developments

During the preparation of this report, there have been multiple developments that affect all three cases analyzed—the most extensive developments obviously pertaining the case of Russia. These developments underline not only the dynamic nature of sanctions as a foreign policy tool and its growing importance as a go-to measure in times of international crisis, but also show how they cannot be viewed in isolation from developments in international affairs at the global, regional, and local level.

6.1 Iran

With regard to Iran, the election of President Biden has opened the possibility of a return to full compliance with the JCPOA of both the USA and Iran, which would result in the lifting of most sanctions against the country. The new administration also presented a chance for European countries to achieve their aim of facilitating JCPOA revival, as their negotiation standpoint had been seriously restricted by President Trump's dismissal of any kind of rapprochement. In March 2021, indirect diplomatic channels to revive the JCPOA commenced between Washington and Tehran through European countries. The Biden administration has refused unilateral sanctions relief but has pursued a "compliance for compliance" approach (Reuters, 2021). Shortly after, Iran also signalled willingness to return to compliance through an established reciprocal mechanism (Bedard, 2022).

While more positive signals were issued by political leaders, Supreme Leader Khamenei repeatedly stated that Iranian compliance would only happen after the US

Supplementary Information The online version contains supplementary material available at https://doi.org/10.1007/978-3-031-17397-4_6.

lifted sanctions. Following this apparent thaw, negotiations resumed in Vienna and the Joint Commission established a working group tasked with the provision of mechanisms to allow rapprochement between the USA and Iran. However, the sixth, seventh, and eighth (currently paused) round of negotiations have not yet produced manifest results (Bedard, 2022).

The victory of conservative candidate Ebrahim Raisi in the presidential elections in June 2021 gave new momentum to the negotiations, as he has claimed to be committed to the revival of the JCPOA. Nonetheless, both Iran and the USA have sent mixed signals concerning their will to de-escalate relations. Iran has consecutively increased its nuclear stockpile, for instance by producing uranium metal enriched up to 20%, operating advanced IR-6 centrifuges and producing uranium enriched up to 20% uranium-235 (Bedard, 2022). The most recent estimates by the IAEA of March 2022 stipulate a stockpile of 3197 kg (33 kg enriched up to 60% purity and 182 kg to 20%) (IAEA, 2022). In addition to nuclear enhancement, Iran has refused the IAEA its oversight rights under the JCPOA and is to date not sharing all data. Tehran had claimed that cameras at the Karaj facility had been damaged in a June cyberattack and subsequently denied inspectors access to reinstall monitoring equipment. This dispute was resolved in December 2021, when an agreement was reached to replace the cameras before the end of the year (Bedard, 2022).

The Biden administration, though committed to JCPOA revival, imposed new sanctions on members of the IRGC and two companies in October 2021. Even though these were unrelated to Iran's nuclear program, new sanctions do not facilitate rapprochement (Office of Foreign Assets Control, 2021c). Tehran also imposed new sanctions on 51 US individuals in January 2022. Washington, however, has also signalled a certain degree of cooperation, as suggested by granting waivers for Russian, Chinese, and European companies working with Iran's civilian nuclear program without being sanctioned in February 2022. Furthermore, while addressing the security threats posed by Iran's launching of the Simorgh space-launch vehicle and a new, 900 mile range solid-fuel missile, the US administration has refrained from further punitive action (Bedard, 2022). Nonetheless, the US treasury designated an oil smuggling and money laundering network led by Islamic Revolutionary Guard Corps-Qods Force (IRGC-QF) official Behnam Shahriyari and former IRGC-QF official Rostam Ghasemi both of which were added to the Specially Designated Nationals List in May 2022 (U.S. Department of the Treasury, 2022d).

Currently, negotiations in Vienna are paused indefinitely, even though both sides have affirmed their commitment to JCPOA revival. Already in February, White House spokesperson Jen Psaki said that without an imminent return to the deal "Iran's ongoing nuclear advances will make it impossible to return to the JCPOA" (The White House, 2022a). Before the Russian invasion of Ukraine, the German Foreign Minister, Iranian Foreign Minister, French Foreign Minister, and White House Press Secretary all issued hopeful statements that talks would shortly conclude successfully (Associated Press, 2022; Hafezi, 2022; Irish, 2022; The White House, 2022b). Even though Moscow and Washington announced to continue cooperation despite Russia's invasion of Ukraine, Russia conditioned its cooperation on JCPOA restoration on guarantees that Western sanctions would not affect its trade with Iran, resulting in the pausing of negotiations on March 11 (Bedard, 2022). While National Security Adviser Jake Sullivan stated it was "unclear" whether the last issues would be resolved (Reuters, 2022c), Iranian Foreign Minister Hossein Amir-Abdollahian believed to be "closer to an agreement in Vienna than ever before" (Reuters, 2022b).

While Ruggiero (2021) argues that Biden's Iran policy is failing, as Tehran has used the strategy of pressure relief to further escalate pressure on its part (even more so than under President Trump), Geranmayeh (2022) emphasizes the current momentum for a return to the deal. As President Biden faces midterm elections in November 2022 and President Raisi has to counter further economic deterioration fueled by the inability to profit from reduced Russian oil prices, considerable push factors to reach an agreement sooner than later exist on both sides. Especially the European partners could use their diplomatic channels to prevent a definite end to the deal.

6.2 North Korea

Finally, the twin burden of sanctions and Covid-19 has put North Korea's economy under immense pressure, as exports to China have significantly decreased (Sang-Hun, 2020). To prevent a Covid-spread, Pyongyang imposed a quarantine on itself, which reduced its international trade immensely, but has refused vaccine donations (Tokola, 2021). It remains to be seen how the recent surge in Covid-19 cases in May 2022 will influence North Korea's behavior. Nonetheless, Kim Jong-un vowed to enhance North Korean nuclear capabilities in January 2021, including the development of tactical nuclear weapons, nuclear-powered submarines, and "small-sized, lightweight" nuclear warheads (The Guardian, 2021).

The election of President Joe Biden was expected to trigger an abandonment of the Trump administration's "go big or go home" approach. After a lengthy policy review, a new course was announced in April 2021. President Biden decided on a middle-ground strategy between the policies of his two predecessors and pursues "a phased agreement that leads to full denuclearization" through a "calibrated, practical approach to diplomacy" (Hudson & Nakashima, 2021). To date, not many more details on Washington's plans have surfaced, however a close alignment with South Korea seems to be a key aspect (Kim, 2022). In May 2021, President Biden and President Moon affirmed their commitment to the denuclearization of the Korean peninsula and inter-Korean dialogue, engagement and cooperation, as codified in the Panmunjom Declaration and the Singapore Joint Statement (The White House, 2021). In February 2022, this alliance was reaffirmed and expanded to incorporate Japan U.S. Department of State (2022a).

Overall, North Korea does not seem to be a policy priority for Washington. While North Korea is focused on its domestic politics, especially tackling Covid-19, US foreign policy is primarily focused on Russia and Ukraine, as well as China. The

Biden administration has committed to unconditional negotiations, while Pyongyang to date is not willing to engage without sanctions relief from Washington (Kim, 2022). At the moment, it is up to North Korea to initiate new negotiations, however without any incentives from the US-side this is unlikely to transpire (Suh, 2021). Currently, the most likely development is the continued nuclear escalation from Pyongyang that cannot be met with any serious international reprimands. This was demonstrated in January 2022, when the DPRK tested seven missiles—more than throughout 2021—and US sanctions proposals in the Security Council were blocked by Russia and China (Council on Foreign Relations, 2022). The latest launch was confirmed to have been an intermediate range ballistic missile, suggested to be the most powerful launch since 2017 and hence "a breaking of the DPRK's announced moratorium in 2018 on launches of this nature, and a clear violation of Security Council resolutions" (UN Secretary-General Guterres, UN News, 2022). Therefore, it remains to be seen, whether North Korea will become a policy priority for the Biden administration, or whether Covid-19 will have such dire effects on the North Korean economy that it will need to pursue sanctions relief.

6.3 Russia

In December 2020, the EU adopted its own "Magnitsky style" sanctions, aimed at dealing with human rights abusers at the global level (Wemer, 2020). This move has been hailed as an important step that would further allow for more cooperation between the EU and the USA on the issue of human rights. Nonetheless, this new sanctions regime has not been used extensively (European Parliamentary Research System, 2021). Currently, 18 persons or entities are sanctioned under this regime, of which 10 are Russian and 3 are North Korean (Council of the European Union, 2021b, 2021d, 2021e). The new sanctions regime's first implementation was in reaction to the poisoning of Alexei Navalny, as was made clear by the High Representative for Foreign Affairs and Security, Josep Borrell, at the Foreign Affairs Council in February 2021: "In response to the events around the situation of Mr. Navalny we reached a political agreement to impose restrictive measures against those responsible for his arrest, sentencing and persecution. For the first time ever we will make use of the EU Global Human Rights Regime to this end" (Council of the European Union, 2021a). In the USA, the poisoning of Navalny triggered chemical and biological weapons act sanctions, the designation of seven government officials under Executive Order 13382 "Blocking Property of Weapons of Mass Destruction Proliferators and Their Supporters," and the addition of six entities to the "Countering America's Adversaries Through Sanctions Act Section 231 List of Specified Persons" (U.S. Department of State, 2021).

Succeeding these new sanctions, the EU added several Russian entities to the sanctions list under Council Regulation 269/2014 ("concerning restrictive measures in respect of actions undermining or threatening the territorial integrity, sovereignty and independence of Ukraine" (Council of the European Union, 2021c)) in March,

September, October, and December 2021, as well as 21 February 2022. However, no new foundations for sanctions imposition were constructed throughout 2021.

In the USA, sanctions against Russian entities were continuously extended throughout 2021. Russian entities were added to the Entity List designating export administration regulations due to actions "contrary to the national security or foreign policy interests of the United States" (Bureau of Industry and Security, 2021a, 2021b, 2021c), as well as the Specially Designated Nationals and Blocked Persons List (Office of Foreign Assets Control, 2021a, 2021b, 2021d). The US government under President Biden also issued two Executive Orders tightening the sanctions regime and reflecting the more rigorous Russia policy of the current administration. In April 2021, President Biden declared certain activities of the Russian government, including attempts to influence elections, malicious cyber-activities, transnational corruption and violations of international law, an "extraordinary threat to the national security, foreign policy, and economy of the United States" and subsequently enforced the blocking of property and interests in property of any persons involved in such activity (Executive Office of the President, 2021a). In Directive 1 under EO 14024 the Russian Central Bank, National Wealth Fund and Ministry of Finance were determined as "political subdivisions, agencies, or instrumentalities" of the Russian government and US financial institutions were prohibited from participating in the primary market for ruble and non-ruble denominated bonds issued by these institutions or lending ruble or non-ruble denominated funds to them (U. S. Department of the Treasury, 2021). These restrictions were further tightened through EO 14039 in August 2021 that blocked "property with respect to certain Russian energy export lines" (Executive Office of the President, 2021c). Additionally, Russian entities were affected by EO 14308 "blocking property of additional persons contributing to the situation in Belarus," which was issued in response to the Belarusian presidential elections in August 2021 and the sustained oppressive activities in the country (Executive Office of the President, 2021b). The US sanctions policy toward Russia under President Biden was hence more comprehensive in both qualitative and quantitative terms than that of the EU. In both case studies however, the sanctions regime changed drastically after the Russian invasion of Ukraine in February 2022.

6.3.1 Russia's Invasion of Ukraine

Russia's invasion of Ukraine resulted in a uniquely comprehensive international sanctions regime against the country (Meister & Jalilvand, 2022); according to Statista (2022), there are currently over 10,900 restrictive measures in place against Russia, of which over 8000 were imposed after February 22, 2022. The European Union has adopted six sanctions packages since the end of February that are "designed to cripple the Kremlin's ability to finance the war, impose clear economic and political costs on Russia's political elite responsible for invasion and diminish its economic base" (European Commission, 2022a). The first three packages were already passed in February (23, 25, 28), the fourth was passed on 15 March, the fifth on 8 April, and the sixth on 3 June (European Council, 2022). To date, 1158 individuals and 98 entities have been targeted by restrictive measures in the form of travel bans, asset freezes and fund provision prohibitions due to their involvement in the "undermining or threatening the territorial integrity, sovereignty and independence of Ukraine." The sanctioned persons include political representatives such as President Putin and further key decision-makers in both Russia and Belarus. In terms of the financial sector, Russia's access to the European capital market and its own reserves in the EU has been subsequently reduced. Transactions with the Russian Central Bank as well as several other Russian and Belarusian banks have been prohibited and assets have been frozen. Selected Russian state-owned enterprises have also been included in transaction bans, as has the export of any EU currency or transferable security. Furthermore, advisory services to wealthy Russian citizens concerning asset management are illegal and Russian nationals and entities have been excluded from procurement contracts in the EU. Key Russian banks were already excluded from the financial messaging system SWIFT in early March (European Commission, 2022a).

The EU aims to minimize the income of the Russian state by prohibiting the import of steel products, cement, rubber products, wood, spirits, liquor, and high-end seafood. Export bans were imposed on luxury goods, quantum computing, advanced semiconductors, sensitive machinery, transportation, chemicals, jet fuel, and fuel additives. Most notably, a complete import ban of all Russian seaborne crude oil and petroleum products was imposed in the last sanctions package, covering 90% of current oil imports from Russia. All forms of Russian coal also underlie an import ban. According to the European Commission, the entirety of coal import bans amounts to 8 billion euros of lost revenue per year. The sanctions list contains predominantly individuals and entities crucial to the military and defense sector of the Russian Federation, limiting access to vital technologies in the military efforts. Restrictions have also been imposed on the transport sector; the export, sale or transfer of all aircraft, aircraft parts and equipment to Russia, as well as providing repair or maintenance services to aircraft have been banned. The closure of the EU airspace to Russian aircrafts was one of the first responses and was imposed at the end of February. Additionally, the export of maritime navigation goods and radio communication technology was restricted, the EU road network has been closed to Russian and Belarusian cargo transport and Russian-flagged vessels are prohibited from entering EU ports. Russian disinformation actors, most prominently RT and Sputnik, have also been sanctioned for constituting "a direct threat to the EU's public order and security" (European Commission, 2022a, 2022b).

The USA have closely coordinated their restrictive actions against the Russian Federation with the European Union (and the G7) and have imposed a very similar sanctions regime. The USA has restricted transactions of major Russian financial institutions, including Sberbank and VTB Bank, Russia's two largest financial institutions and their subsidiaries, the Russian Central Bank, the National Wealth Bank and the Ministry of Finance, limiting Russia's ability to acquire capital and deploying its international reserves. (U.S. Department of State, 2022c, 2022d). After discovering the supposed war crimes committed by the Russian forces in Bucha and other Ukrainian towns, financial sector sanctions were expanded to full blocking sanctions on Sberbank, Alfabank, Russia's largest private bank, and Russian state-owned enterprises, including Russian television stations viewed in the USA (The White House Briefing Room, 2022c). Additionally, new investment in Russia has been prohibited for any US person (The White House Briefing Room, 2022c) and US persons are forbidden to provide accounting, trust and corporate formation, and management consulting services in relation to the Russian economy (Blinken, 2022b).

US sanctions have also targeted the defense and technology sectors of the Russian economy, imposing restrictive measures on individuals and entities involved in the procurement of defense and technology and blocking vessels of maritime shipping companies transporting military equipment for the Russian government (U.S. Department of State, 2022b; Blinken, 2022a). Immediately after the Russian invasion, the Department of Commerce imposed comprehensive export controls restricting access, especially to vital technologies. The export controls also apply to foreign items produced using US equipment, software, or blueprints (Bureau of Industry and Security, 2022a). Over 100 individuals and entities in the aerospace, maritime, and defense sector have been added to the Department of Commerce's Entity List (listing all foreign entities with restricted trade regulations) (Bureau of Industry and Security, 2022b). Additionally, possibilities to generate revenue have been restricted through banning the import of Russian oil, liquefied natural gas and coal, the import of Russian fish, seafood, alcoholic beverages and non-industrial diamonds, the export of luxury goods to the Russian Federation, and the supply of US-dollar denominated banknotes to Russia or any person in Russia (The White House Briefing Room, 2022a, 2022b). Hundreds of individuals, most notably Russian elites and their families including the Russian President, Foreign Minister and Duma members, have been sanctioned for their role in enabling the unlawful invasion of Ukraine (U.S. Department of the Treasury, 2022a, 2022b, 2022c; U.S. Department of State, 2022b; Blinken, 2022a, 2022c).

The Russian Federation has responded with partially reciprocal measures. Russia has imposed capital controls, prohibiting the transfer of hard currency abroad (Hirtenstein, 2022) and the export of telecom, medical, auto, agricultural, electrical, technological, and certain forestry commodities (Reuters, 2022a). Russia's most important source of revenue stems from the export of oil and gas (Tabuchi, 2022). While both the EU and USA have banned the import of Russian oil, Russian natural gas has not yet been sanctioned. Nonetheless, Russia itself has imposed restrictive measures on its gas exports. Russian President Putin signed a decree on 31 March stipulating a new provision for foreign buyers to pay for Russian gas in roubles despite the contractual demand of US dollars (Nasr & Trevelyan, 2022). To date, Russia has suspended gas supplies to Bulgaria, Poland, the Netherlands, Denmark, and Finland for refusal to pay in roubles (TASS, 2022a, 2022c). Additionally, Russia has prohibited transactions with 31 foreign energy companies in the EU and USA as a retaliatory measure (TASS, 2022b). Further retaliatory measures include the blacklisting of US citizens, including Vice President Harris and Meta CEO Mark

Zuckerberg. This list was expanded in May to include further 963 US citizens, including President Biden and Secretary of State Blinken, and again in June to include 61 US officials and executives, permanently prohibiting their entry to the Russian Federation (TASS, 2022d; Reuters, 2022d). Finally, Russia has also enacted a law making the "spreading of false information" on the invasion ("special operation") illegal. While this is essentially a domestic law aimed at message control, it also includes blocking the access to foreign-based Russian-language media outlets as well as Facebook (Troianovski & Safronova, 2022).

The effect of Western sanctions on the Russian economy cannot yet be determined, as it is unclear how long sanctions will prevail and what their long-term effect will be. According to the US government, approximately 1000 businesses have left Russia following international sanctions (The White House Briefing Room, 2022d). The International Monetary Fund estimates that the Russian economy will shrink by 8.5%, inflation will be at 24% (which is well above the inflation prognosis of the Russian Central Bank), and unemployment will reach 9.6% over the course of 2022. While the rouble experienced a depreciation of 60% in the first 2 weeks after the invasion, the Russian response (capital controls, increase of interest rates, closing of stock markets) allowed for a recovery and return of some stability that is, however, dependent on high interest rates and capital controls. Russia's imports are projected to reduce by 25% throughout 2022 and the inaccessibility of foreign production parts and consumer goods, as well as exodus of foreign companies, is anticipated to result in massive job loss (Nelson, 2022). Russian airlines have reported a loss of almost 3 million passengers, Russia currently only has two functioning automobile assembling plants, real incomes have declined compared to the first quarter of 2021 (monthly data on real income is no longer published) and consumer behavior has shifted away from luxury items (Gontmakher, 2022). All of these developments amount to a setback of 15 years in economic development in Russia (The White House Briefing Room, 2022d).

Nonetheless, rise in global energy prices has led to a Russian current account surplus that could exceed $250 billion in 2022 (Nelson, 2022). In the first 100 days of the war, Russia gained 93 billion euros from energy exports, of which the EU imported 61%. Even though import volumes fell, export prices are 60% higher on average than 1 year ago, and fossil fuel revenues are estimated to exceed Russian spending on the invasion of Ukraine (Myllyvirta et al., 2022). This seems to suggest that any Russian policy changes will happen later rather than sooner and currently there is nothing suggesting any such changes. According to Chris Weafer (cited in Rosenberg, 2022), the resilience Russia has built up against sanctions due to their continued exposure and adaptation to them since 2014 is the reason why its economy has not yet collapsed. Hufbauer (cited in Quinn, 2022) argues that sanctions against great powers have no realistic chance of changing the policy course of a leader and that sanctions as a policy response to an invasion are primarily designed to signal criticism and a sense of action toward the domestic population.

The current sanctions regime will, however, definitely impact the global economy. Global supply chains, already strained by the pandemic, have been disrupted, prices have increased and global economic growth is projected to reduce from 6.1%

in 2021 to 3.6% in 2022 (a culmination of pandemic and sanctions) (Nelson, 2022). Global energy flows are already changing; Russia is exporting more to India and China and Europe is importing more from West Africa and Latin America (Vakulenko, 2022). Without any clear timeline on the duration, it is difficult to determine whether the sanctions, especially in the energy sector, will have other effects such as a return to global economic blocks, new alliances, economic agreements, or a global estrangement from the dollar (Nelson, 2022). However, this unprecedented international sanctions regime will undoubtedly effect the economic reality not only of Russians, but of people all over the world.

Chapter 7
Conclusion

The application of sanctions as a foreign policy tool has developed considerably, particularly over the last three decades. Many states and international organizations seem to have embraced sanctions as their go-to tool when dealing with international crisis which has resulted in a vastly increased frequency of sanctions-usage since the 1990s. Not only has the frequency of sanctions increased drastically, sanctions are also used to address a much broader range of foreign policy challenges, including terrorism, human rights violations, cyber security as well as more traditional challenges like nuclear proliferation and territorial integrity. As such, sanctions have also been applied against a much more diverse set of actors. While still most sanctions regimes are imposed against state actors, they are also increasingly applied to terrorist organizations, financial institutions, and even individuals. These more recent sanctions have sought to complement or supplement the more comprehensive sanctions regimes traditionally employed.

In order to analyze these general trends in more detail, this report sought to investigate a number of aspects in the cases of the sanctions regimes imposed against Russia, Iran, and North Korea. These cases are of particular interest to the study of sanctions not only because they are concerned with some of the most important challenges to international security, but also because these cases have undergone significant changes both from the sanctions imposing countries and the targeted countries. Furthermore, while these cases share some important characteristics, they also offer many key differences between them, which makes a comparing these cases worthwhile. With this in mind, this report has sought to provide analysis and insights into key features of these three sanctions regimes.

This report first sought to identify which objectives the sender countries were pursuing with the imposition of sanctions. The section on objectives of sanctions not

---

Supplementary Information The online version contains supplementary material available at https://doi.org/10.1007/978-3-031-17397-4_7.

only showed how senders seek to achieve a wide array of goals with their sanctions regime, but also that these goals not only differ between states part of the same sanctioning coalition, they further can change over time depending on shifting domestic political priorities. The most notable example for the former is the diverging objectives of the USA and the EU when it comes to sanctions imposed against Russia. While both actors are interested in strongly responding to Russian action in Eastern Ukraine and on Crimea, the EU has carefully sought to balance its response in order not to inflict too much self-harm on its own Member States economies that are far more reliant on trade with Russia than the USA is. In addition, the EU has chosen to closely link sanctions relief to progress in the Minsk II process, while the USA has not provided clear guidelines of how a change in Russian behavior in Ukraine would be reciprocated by the USA. This differing approach to the situation in Eastern Ukraine and Crimea has since led to considerable tensions between the USA and the EU. The most notable example for the latter insight is the change in US behavior toward Iran after the election of Donald Trump as US President. The USA leaving the JCPOA, a deal that has been mostly hailed as a successful example of how sanctions can support finding a solution to an international security crisis, and imposing its unilateral strategy of maximum pressure against Iran exemplifies a significant change in objectives caused by changes in the political situation in a sender country.

The second section of this report was dedicated to giving a detailed and up-to-date description of the specific sanctions measures imposed by the UN, the EU, and the USA in all three cases. Most importantly the section highlighted the dynamic nature of sanctions. Particularly the cases of Iran and North Korea underlined how sanctions regimes constantly need to evolve in the face of changes in the international system as well as developments in the targeted countries. Furthermore, the section has shown that while the UN Security Council can be one of the most important actors to create coherent sanctions regimes, it is at times not flexible enough to adjust to newer developments, due to the time-consuming but necessary consensus building between the permanent members of the Security Council. In contrast, the section showed that both the EU and the USA are becoming increasingly willing to impose sanctions measures in response to a broader set of security challenges.

The third part of the report sought to assess how the sanctions regimes had affected the targeted countries. In general, in all three cases the sanctions imposed had an effect on the targeted economies. However, in all three cases the effects can only be considered relatively small, either because they were not far reaching enough, e.g. the self-imposed limits of EU sanctions against the Russian energy sector, because the interdependencies between the countries were limited (e.g., US trade with Russia is very limited, hence sanctions only affected Russian trade marginally), or because exposure to the global economy was already almost non-existent, as in the case of North Korea. Secondly, while there has been a negative economic effect on all three countries during the time period analyzed, most of it has to be attributed to other external developments in the international economy, in particular the developments in global oil prices. Even more so, while many of the sanctions were designed to be specifically targeted at entities and

7 Conclusion

persons that are directly involved with the sanctioned behavior, there seems to be evidence that the elites in question were able to mostly avoid direct negative effects of the sanctions. Furthermore, a big part of the burden imposed through sanctions on countries is carried by the general population rather than the decision-makers in the governments of Iran, North Korea, and Russia. In addition, while there is some evidence that sanctions have negatively affected the targeted economies, the sanctions so far have failed to achieve their political goals. Russia's position in Eastern Ukraine and Crimea has remained relatively unchanged since the beginning of the sanctions regime in 2014. Similarly, sanctions have so far also failed to stop North Korea's nuclear proliferation activities and its program to develop ballistic missiles. An exception to this is how sanctions played an integral role in bringing Iran to the negotiation table that resulted in the drafting of the JCPOA. However, with the USA unilaterally leaving the deal, the agreement has been put under a lot of pressure and Iran has in response announced to start enriching uranium at a higher level than agreed upon in the JCPOA and to exceed its enriched uranium stockpile (BBC News, 2021a).

Finally, the fourth section investigated how Russia, Iran, and North Korea reacted to these sanctions measures and which countermeasures these three countries imposed. The section showcased how the targets of sanctions have adapted to them. It further underlines how stronger economies can leverage a larger number of measures in dealing with the negative consequences imposed by sanctions, as could be observed in the Russian case, in which Russia even went as far as to impose travel restrictions and import bans against European countries. The Russian case also underlined the importance of having a broad multilateral coalition that partakes in imposing sanctions, as Russia was able to diversify its trade portfolio in the face of trade restrictions with the EU and the USA, albeit with only limited success. In contrast, North Korea and Iran had only limited options in responding to the sanctions imposed by the UN, the EU, and the USA. Hence, Iran and North Korea mostly focused their efforts on seeking illicit ways to avoid sanctions, such as illicit maritime activity and seeking to hide transactions behind opaque business and financial structures. In addition, both countries also sought to adjust its domestic economy to be less reliant on trade and hence to be less vulnerable to sanctions. While both North Korea and Iran have sought to modernize and diversify its economy regardless of sanctions, they have only made limited progress on it, limiting their ways to respond to sanctions.

This in-depth study of sanctions against Russia, North Korea, and Iran suggests a number of important aspects that can further inform the use of sanctions as a foreign policy tool. First, while sanctions can have an immediate economic effect, it seems that for this economic effect to translate into a political effect the costs imposed have to be maintained and hence sanctions should be viewed as mid- to long-term tools. This also necessitates to view sanctions not as a strategy in its own right but as a tool that has to be carefully balanced with other available foreign policy tools. Second, sanctions measures seem to be more likely to have the intended effect if they are linked to specific and clearly articulated goals. In this regard, the sender countries should put special emphasis on communicating its expectations of the target country as well as specific steps that could lead to a reduction or lifting of sanctions. In line with this, sender countries should seek to limit their goals to realistically achievable change in behavior, particularly when dealing with countries that are important players in the global economy. Third, sender countries need to understand the imposition of sanctions as a dynamic process between multiple actors. Given that targeted states will seek to minimize the costs imposed by sanctions, they will seek to adjust to circumvent sanctions. Hence, sanctions regimes need to be closely monitored and sender countries need to be flexible in order to successfully adjust the sanctions measures to reflect the new circumstances. Furthermore, senders should also be flexible and proportional in reacting to positive steps taken by the target country. Finally, sanctions seem to be more effective when they are based on a broad multilateral coalition. In the best case they are mandated by the United Nations Security Council and hence almost universal and mandatory. However, as this report has shown, the implementation of UN sanctions resolutions needs to be closely monitored and regularly updated.

As a final note it has to be mentioned that all three cases analyzed in this report are still developing. This leaves a lot of uncertainty about how these international crisis will further develop. Depending on a number of factors, some situations may de-escalate, while others may further escalate, even risking military confrontations between the actors involved. However, given the current trajectory, as well as the strategic interests by all countries involved, escalation to such a point seems rather unlikely. Even despite the Russian invasion of Ukraine, military action by NATO countries is not probable from a current perspective. Nonetheless, Russian military escalation in Ukraine did not seem likely before the actual invasion, as Russia had already achieved its goals if halting a deeper integration of Ukraine into the EU as well as securing Russian access to the Black Sea. This showcases that any such predictions might prove irrelevant in the future and it is difficult to ascertain the outcome of the conflict.

For how the situation in North Korea develops a number of factors will play an important role. Most notably it will depend on if North Korea will adopt a more provocative stance again and if China will change its strategy if North Korea continues to make progress on its nuclear and ballistic missile programs. Another factor will be how US President Biden chooses to engage the situation. Currently the most likely scenario for the USA is to return to the "strategic patience" approach, with sanctions seeking to increase pressure on North Korea while communicating the willingness to negotiate if North Korea shows reasonable commitment. Military intervention, while sometimes mentioned as a viable option, does not seem to be very likely, as both US allies, most notably South Korea, and adversaries such as China are strongly opposed to a military confrontation as it could potentially involve the use of nuclear weapons by North Korea.

If the situation with Iran will improve or deteriorate will depend to a large degree on if the USA is able to rejoin the JCPOA and if Iran will return into full compliance with the deal. Out of the three cases discussed in this report, the confrontation with Iran poses the highest risk of escalating. Particularly the tensions between Iran and the USA are posing a real risk of spiraling out of control, as was the case between

7 Conclusion

December 2019 and January 2020 when direct conflict erupted between the two countries. While aggressions were somewhat limited, it still constituted a significant risk of further escalating into full war.[1] Hence, if there will be another period of heightened tensions will depend on US President Biden's approach to Iran and on if the two countries will be able to resolve issues surrounding the US rejoining the JCPOA. However, even if the issues around the JCPOA will be resolved, which will certainly lower the risk of conflict, this will not necessarily lead to the resolution of other issues, such as Iran's regional military involvement or its human rights record. These issues will continue to strain relations with Iran. Therefore, it is also unlikely that sanctions will cease to be a central element in the relationship with Iran.

Given the uncertainty and complexity surrounding the developments in all three cases discussed in this report, it will be pertinent for academics and policymakers alike to continue to closely monitor them.

---

[1] Aggressions included rocket attacks on Iraqi military facilities, where US forces were also based, by Iranian proxy actors. The most notable US escalation was the targeted killing of Iranian Revolutionary Guard Corps Quds Force (IRGC-QF) Commander Qasem Soleimani.

References

Ahn, D. P., & Ludema, R. D. (2019). *The sword and the shield: The economics of targeted sanctions* (CESifo Working paper No. 7620). Center for Economic Studies and IFO Institute. http://hdl.handle.net/10419/198980
Allen, S. H. (2005). The determinants of economic sanctions success and failure. *International Interactions, 31*(2), 117–138.
Ashford, E. (2016). Not-so-smart sanctions: The failure of western restrictions against Russia. *Foreign Affairs, 95*(1), 114–123.
Associated Press. (2020, April 16). Ukrainian forces and Russia-backed rebels exchange prisoners. *AP News*. https://apnews.com/article/a9a751b28527ba0cbd36166cdecee06b
Associated Press. (2022, February 10). German FM says Iran nuclear talks entering "final phase". *AP News*. https://apnews.com/article/yair-lapid-israel-middle-east-iran-tel-aviv-6804bfe55f5fe6ebbf84294de1834c57
Baldwin, D. A. (2000). The sanctions debate and the logic of choice. *International Security, 24*(3), 80–107.
Bapat, N. A., Heinrich, T., Kobayashi, Y., & Clifton Morgan, T. (2013). Determinants of sanctions effectiveness: Sensitivity analysis using new data. *International Interactions, 39*(1), 79–98.
Bapat, N. A., & Kwon, B. (2015). When are sanctions effective? A bargaining and enforcement framework. *International Organization, 69*(1), 131–162.
Barber, J. (1979). Economic sanctions as a policy instrument. *International Affairs, 55*(3), 367–384.
Barseghyan, G. (2019). *Sanctions and counter-sanctions: What did they do?* (Vol. 24, BOFIT discussion papers). Bank of Finland, BOFIT Institute for Economies in Transition.
BBC News. (2021a, January 1). Iran nuclear crisis: Tehran to enrich uranium to 20%, IAEA says. *BBC News*. https://www.bbc.com/news/world-middle-east-55509048
BBC News. (2021b, January 5). South Korea to send delegation after Iran seizes tanker. *BBC News*. https://www.bbc.com/news/world-asia-55540507
Bedard, J. (2022, April). *Timeline of nuclear diplomacy with Iran*. Arms Control Association. Retrieved May 15, 2022, from https://www.armscontrol.org/factsheets/Timeline-of-Nuclear-Diplomacy-With-Iran#2020
Blanc, J., & Weiss, A. S. (2019, April 3). *U.S. sanctions on Russia: Congress should go back to fundamentals*. Carnegie Endowment for International Peace. https://carnegieendowment.org/2019/04/03/u.s.-sanctions-on-russia-congress-should-go-back-to-fundamentals-pub-78755
Blanchard, B. (2012, January 4). China repeats opposition to unilateral sanctions on Iran. *Reuters*. https://www.reuters.com/article/us-china-iran-usa/china-repeats-opposition-to-unilateral-sanctions-on-iran-idUSTRE8030SI20120104

Blanchard, J. F., & Ripsman, N. M. (1999). Asking the right question: When do economic sanctions work best? *Security Studies, 9*(1–2), 219–253.

Blinken, A. J. (2022a, March 31). *Additional sanctions on Russia's technology companies and cyber actors* [Press statement]. U.S. Department of State. https://www.state.gov/additional-sanctions-on-russias-technology-companies-and-cyber-actors/

Blinken, A. J. (2022b, May 8). *Targeting Russia's financial, defense, and marine sectors and promoting accountability for Russian and Belarusian military officials* [Press statement]. U.-S. Department of State. https://www.state.gov/targeting-russias-financial-defense-and-marine-sectors-and-promoting-accountability-for-russian-and-belarusian-military-officials/

Blinken, A. J. (2022c, June 2). *Targeting Russia's oligarchs and vessels* [Press statement]. U.-S. Department of State. https://www.state.gov/targeting-russias-oligarchs-and-vessels/

Bozorgmehr, N., & England, A. (2020, April 15.) Iran embarks on biggest IPO as economy struggles. *Financial Times.* https://www.ft.com/content/86eaf33d-699f-4a71-8a94-67225044c6a6

Brzozowski, A. (2020 April 1). EU's INSTEX mechanism facilitates first transaction with pandemic-hit Iran. *Euractiv.* https://www.euractiv.com/section/global-europe/news/eus-instex-mechanism-facilitates-first-transaction-with-pandemic-hit-iran/

Bueno de Mesquita, B. (2005). *The logic of political survival* (1st ed.). MIT Press.

Bureau of Industry and Security. (2021a, March 4). *Addition of certain entities to the entity list; correction of existing entries on the entity list* [Final rule]. 86 FR 12529. https://www.federalregister.gov/documents/2021/03/04/2021-04505/addition-of-certain-entities-to-the-entity-list-correction-of-existing-entries-on-the-entity-list

Bureau of Industry and Security. (2021b, July 12). *Addition of certain entities to the entity list; revision of existing entry on the entity list; removal of entity from the unverified list; and addition of entity to the military end-user (meu) list* [Final rule]. 86 FR 36496. https://www.federalregister.gov/documents/2021/07/12/2021-14656/addition-of-certain-entities-to-the-entity-list-revision-of-existing-entry-on-the-entity-list

Bureau of Industry and Security. (2021c, July 19). *Addition of entities and revision of entry on the entity list* [Final rule]. 86 FR 37901. https://www.federalregister.gov/documents/2021/07/19/2021-15362/addition-of-entities-and-revision-of-entry-on-the-entity-list

Bureau of Industry and Security. (2022a, February 24). *Commerce implements sweeping restrictions on exports to Russia in response to further invasion of Ukraine* [Press release]. https://bis.doc.gov/index.php/documents/about-bis/newsroom/press-releases/2914-2022-02-24-bis-russia-rule-press-release-and-tweets-final/file

Bureau of Industry and Security. (2022b, April 1). *Commerce adds 120 entities in Russia and Belarus to the entity list, further limiting the Russian and Belarusian militaries' access to items that support aggression against Ukraine* [Press release]. U.S. Department of Commerce. https://www.commerce.gov/news/press-releases/2022/04/commerce-adds-120-entities-russia-and-belarus-entity-list-further

Bush, G. W. (2002, January 29). *The President's state of the Union address.* The White House. https://georgewbush-whitehouse.archives.gov/news/releases/2002/01/20020129-11.html

Bush, G. W. (2006, January 31). *The President's state of the Union address.* The White House. https://georgewbush-whitehouse.archives.gov/stateoftheunion/2006/

Cooper, H., & Sanger, D. (2007, June 16). Iran strategy stirs debate at white house. *The New York Times.* https://www.nytimes.com/2007/06/16/washington/16diplo.html?ref=todayspaper

Council of the European Union. (2014, March 17). *EU adopts restrictive measures against actions threatening Ukraine's territorial integrity* [Press release]. https://www.consilium.europa.eu/media/28726/141603.pdf

Council of the European Union. (2019a, July 15). *North Korea: EU renews its autonomous sanctions on individuals and entities* [Press release]. https://www.consilium.europa.eu/en/press/press-releases/2019/07/15/north-korea-eu-renews-its-autonomous-sanctions-on-individuals-and-entities/

References

Council of the European Union. (2019b, December 20). *Council decision (CFSP) 2019/2192* (Vol. 62). https://eur-lex.europa.eu/eli/dec/2019/2192/oj/eng

Council of the European Union. (2020, March 13). *Council decision (CFSP) 2020/399* (Vol. 63). https://eur-lex.europa.eu/legal-content/EN/TXT/?uri=celex:32020D0399

Council of the European Union. (2021a, February 22). *Foreign affairs council, 22 February 2021*. European Council–Council of the European Union. https://www.consilium.europa.eu/en/meetings/fac/2021/02/22/

Council of the European Union. (2021b, March 2). Council implementing regulation (EU) 2021/371. *Official Journal of the European Union*, LI 71/1. https://eur-lex.europa.eu/legal-content/EN/TXT/?uri=uriserv%3AOJ.LI.2021.071.01.0001.01.ENG&toc=OJ%3AL%3A2021%3A0 71I%3ATOC

Council of the European Union. (2021c, March 12). Council implementing regulation (EU) 2021/446. *Official Journal of the European Union*, L 87/19. https://eur-lex.europa.eu/legal-content/EN/TXT/?uri=uriserv%3AOJ.L_.2021.087.01.0019.01.ENG&toc=OJ%3AL%3A2021%3A0 87%3ATOC

Council of the European Union. (2021d, March 22). Council implementing regulation (EU) 2021/478. *Official Journal of the European Union*, L 99 I/1. https://eur-lex.europa.eu/legal-content/EN/TXT/PDF/?uri=OJ:L:2021:099I:FULL&from=EN

Council of the European Union. (2021e, December 13). Council implementing regulation (EU) 2021/2195. *Official Journal of the European Union*, L 445 I/10. https://eur-lex.europa.eu/legal-content/EN/TXT/PDF/?uri=OJ:L:2021:445I:FULL&from=DE

Council on Foreign Relations. (2022). Timeline: North Korean nuclear negotiations. *Council on Foreign Relations*. Retrieved May 15, 2022, from https://www.cfr.org/media/31705/modal

Crozet, M., & Hinz, J. (2020). Friendly fire: The trade impact of the Russia sanctions and counter-sanctions. *Economic Policy, 35*(101), 97–146.

Dorussen, H. (2001). Mixing carrots with sticks: Evaluating the effectiveness of positive incentives. *Journal of Peace Research, 38*(2), 251–262.

Drezner, D. W. (2003). The hidden hand of economic coercion. *International Organization, 57*(3), 643–659.

Drezner, D. W. (2011). Sanctions sometimes smart: Targeted sanctions in theory and practice. *International Studies Review, 13*(1), 96–108.

Drezner, D. W. (2015). Targeted sanctions in a world of global finance. *International Interactions, 41*(4), 755–764. https://doi.org/10.1080/03050629.2015.1041297

Drury, A. C. (2001). Sanctions as coercive Diploimacy: The U.S. president's decision to initiate economic sanctions. *Political Research Quarterly, 54*(3), 485–508.

Dumbrell, J. (2007). *The Bush administration, US public diplomacy and Iran (working paper)*. Durham University, School of Government and International Affairs. https://dro.dur.ac.uk/4123/

EEAS. (2013, October 14). *The European Union and Iran* [Fact sheet]. European Union External Action Service. https://www.europarl.europa.eu/meetdocs/2009_2014/documents/d-ir/dv/eu_iran_factsheet_14o/eu_iran_factsheet_14oct.pdf

European Commission. (2020). *Agri-food trade statistical factsheet: European Union–Russia* [Factsheet]. https://ec.europa.eu/info/sites/info/files/food-farming-fisheries/farming/documents/agrifood-russia_en.pdf

European Commission. (2021, January 18). *Parliamentary questions: Answer given by high representative/vice-president Borrell on behalf of the European Commission* (question reference E-005506/2020). https://www.europarl.europa.eu/doceo/document/E-9-2020-005506-ASW_EN.html

European Commission. (2022a). *EU sanctions against Russia following the invasion of Ukraine*. European Commission. Retrieved June 20, 2022, from https://ec.europa.eu/info/strategy/priorities-2019-2024/stronger-europe-world/eu-solidarity-ukraine/eu-sanctions-against-russia-following-invasion-ukraine_en

European Commission. (2022b, March 2). *Ukraine: Sanctions on Kremlin-backed outlets* [Press release]. https://ec.europa.eu/commission/presscorner/detail/en/ip_22_1490

European Council. (2022). EU response to Russia's invasion of Ukraine. *European Council–Council of the European Union*. Retrieved June 21, 2022, from https://www.consilium.europa.eu/en/policies/eu-response-ukraine-invasion/

European Parliament. (2017, September 20). Russia's and the EU's sanctions: Economic and trade effects, compliance and the way forward. *Think Tank European Parliament*. https://www.europarl.europa.eu/thinktank/en/document.html?reference=EXPO_STU(2017)603847

European Parliamentary Research System. (2021). *Global human rights sanctions. Mapping Magnitsky laws: The US, Canadian, UK and EU approach* [Briefing]. https://www.europarl.europa.eu/RegData/etudes/BRIE/2021/698791/EPRS_BRI(2021)698791_EN.pdf

Executive Office of the President. (2021a, April 15). *Executive order 14024 of April 15, 2021 blocking property with respect to specified harmful foreign activities of the government of the Russian federation* [Executive Order]. Vol. 86, No 73. https://www.govinfo.gov/content/pkg/FR-2021-04-19/pdf/2021-08098.pdf

Executive Office of the President. (2021b, August 9). *Executive order 14038 of August 9, 2021 blocking property of additional persons contributing to the situation in Belarus* [Executive Order]. Vol. 86, No. 152 https://home.treasury.gov/system/files/126/14038.pdf

Executive Office of the President. (2021c, August 20). *Executive order 14039 of August 20, 2021 blocking property with respect to certain Russian energy export pipelines* [Executive Order]. Vol. 86, No. 161. https://home.treasury.gov/system/files/126/14039.pdf

Felbermayr, G., Kirilakha, A., Syropoulos, C., Yalcin, E., & Yotov, Y. (2020). The global sanctions data base. *European Economic Review, 129*, 103561. https://doi.org/10.1016/j.euroecorev.2020.103561

Fischer, S. (2015). European Union sanctions against Russia: Objectives, impacts and next steps. *SWP Comments,* 17. https://www.swp-berlin.org/fileadmin/contents/products/comments/2015C17_fhs.pdf

Foy, H. (2020, January 30). Russia: Adapting to sanctions leaves economy in robust health. *Financial Times*. https://www.ft.com/content/a9b982e6-169a-11ea-b869-0971bffac109

Galtung, J. (1967). On the effects of international economic sanctions, with examples from the case of Rhodesia. *World Politics, 19*(3), 378–416.

Garver, J. (2016, February 8). *China and Iran: An emerging partnership post-sanctions*. Middle East Institute. https://www.mei.edu/publications/china-and-iran-emerging-partnership-post-sanctions

Geranmayeh, E. (2022, April 13). Iran, the US, and the nuclear deal: Biden's chance to remove Trump's poison pill. *European Council on Foreign Relations*. Retrieved May 16, 2022, from https://ecfr.eu/article/iran-the-us-and-the-nuclear-deal-bidens-chance-to-remove-trumps-poison-pill/

Gontmakher, E. (2022, May 31). Russia under sanctions. *Reassessing Russia*. https://www.gisreportsonline.com/r/russia-sanctions/

Giumelli, F. (2011). *Coercing, constraining and signalling: Explaining UN and EU sanctions after the cold war*. ECPR Press.

Gordon, M. R. (2018, May 21). U.S. lays out demands for new Iran deal. *The Wall Street Journal*. Retrieved September 28, 2020, from https://www.wsj.com/articles/mike-pompeo-lays-out-next-steps-on-iran-1526909126

Gould-Davies, N. (2018). Economic effects and political impacts: Assessing western sanctions on Russia. *BOFIT Policy Brief*, 8. https://helda.helsinki.fi/bof/bitstream/handle/123456789/15832/bpb0818.pdf?

Hafezi, P. (2022, February 14). Iran 'is in a hurry' to revive nuclear deal if its interests secured–foreign minister. *Reuters*. https://www.reuters.com/world/middle-east/nuclear-talks-not-dead-end-iran-foreign-ministry-spokesman-says-2022-02-14/

Hedberg, M. (2018). The target strikes back: Explaining countersanctions and Russia's strategy of differentiated retaliation. *Post-Soviet Affairs, 34*(1), 35–54.

References

Hirtenstein, A. (2022, December 28). Putin imposes capital controls including restrictions on external debt payments. *The Wall Street Journal*. https://www.wsj.com/livecoverage/russia-ukraine-latest-news-2022-02-28/card/putin-imposes-capital-controls-including-restrictions-on-external-debt-payments-Kedzfom80kQtl1B7xaRs

Hudson, J., & Nakashima, E. (2021, April 30). Biden administration forges new path on north Korea crisis in wake of trump and Obama failures. *Washington Post, 2021*. https://www.washingtonpost.com/national-security/biden-administration-forges-new-path-on-north-korea-crisis-in-wake-of-trump-and-obama-failures/2021/04/30/c8bef4f2-a9a9-11eb-b166-174b63ea6007_story.html

Hufbauer, G. C., Schott, J. J., & Elliott, K. A. (1990). *Economic sanctions reconsidered: History and current policy* (2nd ed.). Institute for International Economics.

Hufbauer, G. C., Schott, J. J., Elliott, K. A., & Oegg, B. (2007). *Economic sanctions reconsidered* (3rd ed.). Peterson Institute for International Economics.

Human Rights Watch. (2016). *World Report 2016: Iran*. Human Rights Watch.. https://www.hrw.org/world-report/2016/country-chapters/iran

IAEA. (2006, April 28). *Implementation of the NPT safeguards agreement in the Islamic Republic of Iran*. GOV/2006/2. https://www.iaea.org/sites/default/files/gov2006-27.pdf

IAEA, Board of Governors. (2022, March 3). *Verification and monitoring in the Islamic Republic of Iran in light of United Nations Security Council resolution 2231 (2015)*. GOV/2022/4. https://www.iaea.org/sites/default/files/22/03/gov2022-4.pdf

International Monetary Fund. (2019). *Russian federation: 2019 article IV consultation-press release* [staff report]. International Monetary Fund.

Irish, J. (2022, February 16). Decision on nuclear deal days away, ball in Tehran's court: France. *Reuters*. https://www.reuters.com/world/middle-east/decision-iran-nuclear-deal-days-away-ball-tehrans-court-france-2022-02-16/

Jafari, S. (2020, December 3). Biden will have five months to revive the Iran nuclear deal. *Foreign Policy*. https://foreignpolicy.com/2020/12/03/biden-rouhani-zarif-needs-to-move-fast-if-he-wants-a-new-deal-with-iran/

Jin, L. (2010). Analysis on Obama administration's policy adjustment of Iranian nuclear issue. *Journal of Middle Eastern and Islamic Studies (in Asia), 4*(2), 14–31.

Katzman, K. (2020). *Iran sanctions* [CRS Report No. RS20871]. U.S. Congressional Research Service. https://crsreports.congress.gov/product/pdf/RS/RS20871/304

Kern, A. (2009). The origins and use of economic sanctions. In *Economic sanctions: Law and public policy* (pp. 8–29). Palgrave Macmillan.

Kessler, G. (2006, February 16). Rice Asks for $75 million to increase pressure on Iran. *The Washington Post*. https://www.washingtonpost.com/archive/politics/2006/02/16/rice-asks-for-75-million-to-increase-pressure-on-iran/55a7dd64-f51d-4236-8613-9640dd4a3e4f/

Kholodilin, K. A., & Netšunajev, A. (2019). Crimea and punishment: The impact of sanctions on Russian economy and economies of the euro area. *Baltic Journal of Economics, 19*(1), 39–51.

Kim, H. (2022, February 28). A Korean perspective on the Biden administration's North Korea Policy. *Asia Policy Memo*. https://www.stimson.org/2022/a-korean-perspective-on-the-biden-administrations-north-korea-policy/.

Kirshner, J. (2002). Review essay economic sanctions: The state of the art. *Security Studies, 11*(4), 160–179.

Koen, V., & Beom, J. (2020). *North Korea: The last transition economy?* (OECD Economics Department working paper no. 1607). OECD Economics Department. https://www.oecd-ilibrary.org/economics/north-korea-the-last-transition-economy_82dee315-en

Korea Peace Now. (2019, October). *The human costs and gendered impact of sanctions on North Korea*. https://koreapeacenow.org/wp-content/uploads/2019/10/human-costs-and-gendered-impact-of-sanctions-on-north-korea.pdf

Korhonen, I. (2019). Sanctions and counter-sanctions–what are their economic effects in Russia and elsewhere. *BOFIT Policy Brief, 2*. https://helda.helsinki.fi/bof/bitstream/handle/123456789/16334/bpb0219.pdf?sequence=1

Korhonen, I., Simola, H., & Solanko, L. (2018). Sanctions, counter-sanctions and Russia–effects on economy, trade and finance. *BOFIT Policy Brief, 4*. https://helda.helsinki.fi/bof/bitstream/handle/123456789/15510/bpb0418.pdf?sequence=1

Landler, M. (2018, May 8). Trump abandons Iran nuclear deal he long scorned. *The New York Times*. https://www.nytimes.com/2018/05/08/world/middleeast/trump-iran-nuclear-deal.html

Lavrov, S. (2005). *Article of Russian minister of foreign affairs Sergey Lavrov for diplomatic yearbook 2005: The foreign policy outcomes of 2005: Reflections and conclusions*. Ministry of Foreign Affairs of the Russian Federation. https://www.mid.ru/en/web/guest/ukraine/-/asset_publisher/HfLxJk5I2xvu/content/id/418498

Lee, Y. S. (2018). International isolation and regional inequality: Evidence from sanctions on North Korea. *Journal of Urban Economics, 103*, 34–51. http://www.sciencedirect.com/science/article/pii/S0094119017300852

Lindsay, J. M. (1986). Trade sanctions as policy instruments: A re-examination. *International Studies Quarterly, 30*(2), 153–173.

Mangott, G., & Senn, M. (2017). Boycotts, bombs, or bargains? Eine analyse von Strategien im Umgang mit Nordkoreas Nuklearwaffenprogramm. *Zeitschrift für Außen-und Sicherheitspolitik, 10*(1), 13–27.

Marinov, N. (2005). Do economic sanctions destabilize country leaders? *American Journal of Political Science, 49*(3), 564–576.

Martin, M. (2016, April 25). Obama says Russia sanctions must stay in place until Minsk implemented. *Reuters*. https://www.reuters.com/article/us-usa-germany-obama-russia-idUSKCN0XM10K.

Mattis, J., & Tillerson, R. (2017, August 13). We're holding Pyongyang to account: The U.S., its allies and the world are united in our pursuit of a denuclearized Korean Peninsula. *Small Wars Journal*. https://www.wsj.com/articles/were-holding-pyongyang-to-account-1502660253

Medvedev, D. (2010, March 27). *President Dimitry Medvedev's address to the summit meeting of the League of Arab States* [Press statement]. http://en.kremlin.ru/events/president/news/7251

Meister, S., & Jalilvand, D. (2022, June 8). Sanktionen Gegen Russland: Fünf Lehren Aus Dem Fall Iran. *DGAP Policy Brief*. https://dgap.org/de/forschung/publikationen/sanktionen-gegen-russland

Miller, N. L. (2014). The secret success of nonproliferation sanctions. *International Organization, 68*(4), 913–944.

Morgan, T. C., Bapat, N. A., & Kobayashi, Y. (2014). Threat and imposition of economic sanctions 1945–2005: Updating the TIES dataset. *Conflict Management and Peace Science, 31*(5), 541–558.

Myllyvirta, L., Thieriot, H., Ilas, A., & Mykhailenko, O. (2022). *Financing Putin's war: Fossil fuel imports from Russia in the first 100 days of the invasion*. Centre for Research on Energy and Clean Air. https://energyandcleanair.org/wp/wp-content/uploads/2022/06/Financing-Putins-war-100-days_20220613.pdf

Nanto, D. K., & Manyin, M. E. (2010). *China-North Korea relations* [CRS report no. R41043]. U.-S. Congressional Research Service. https://fas.org/sgp/crs/row/R41043.pdf

Nasr, J., & Trevelyan, M. (2022, March 31). Putin tells Europe: Pay in roubles or we'll cut off your gas. *Reuters*. https://www.reuters.com/business/energy/russia-sets-deadline-rouble-gas-payments-europe-calls-it-blackmail-2022-03-31/

Nelson, R. M. (2022). *Russia's war on Ukraine: The economic impact of sanctions*. U.-S. Congressional Research Service. https://crsreports.congress.gov/product/pdf/IF/IF12092#:~:text=Sanctions%20that%20isolate%20Russia%20are,slowdown%20in%20global%20economic%20growth

Nossal, K. R. (1989). International sanctions as international punishment. *International Organization, 43*(2), 301–322.

Office of Foreign Assets Control. (2021a, April 20). *Notice of OFAC sanctions actions* [Notice]. 2021–08087. https://www.federalregister.gov/documents/2021/04/20/2021-08087/notice-of-ofac-sanctions-actions

Office of Foreign Assets Control. (2021b, September 24). *Notice of OFAC sanctions action* [Notice]. 2021–20745. https://www.federalregister.gov/documents/2021/09/24/2021-20745/notice-of-ofac-sanctions-action

Office of Foreign Assets Control. (2021c, October 29). *Treasury sanctions network and individuals in connection with Iran's unmanned aerial vehicle program* [Press release]. https://home.treasury.gov/news/press-releases/jy0443

Office of Foreign Assets Control. (2021d, November 12). *Notice of OFAC sanctions action* [Notice]. 2021–24701. https://www.federalregister.gov/documents/2021/11/12/2021-24701/notice-of-ofac-sanctions-action

O'Sullivan, M. L. (2010). Iran and the great sanctions debate. *The Washington Quarterly, 33*(4), 7–21.

Patterson, R. (2013). EU sanctions on Iran: The European political context. *Middle East Policy, 20*(1), 135–146.

Peksen, D. (2016, June 23). *Authoritarian regimes and economic sanction effectiveness: The case of North Korea*. KEIA academic paper series. Korea Economic Institute of America. http://www.keia.org/sites/default/files/publications/kei_aps_north_korea_sanctions.pdf

Perdum, T. S. (1995, May 1). Clinton to order a trade embargo against Teheran. *The New York Times*. https://crsreports.congress.gov/product/pdf/RS/RS20871/304

Pompeo, M. R. (2018, May 21). *After the deal: A new Iran strategy*. The Heritage Foundation. https://www.heritage.org/defense/event/after-the-deal-new-iran-strategy

Pompeo, M. R. (2020, January 13). *The restoration of deterrence: The Iranian example*. U. S. Department of State. https://www.state.gov/the-restoration-of-deterrence-the-iranian-example/

Portela, C. (2005). Where and why does the EU impose sanctions? *Politique européenne, 3*, 83–111.

Portela, C. (2015). EU strategies to tackle the Iranian and north Korean nuclear issues. In S. Blavoukos, D. Bourantonis, & C. Portela (Eds.), *The EU and the non-proliferation of nuclear weapons: Strategies, policies, actions* (pp. 188–204). Palgrave Macmillan.

Portela, C. (2016). Are European union sanctions "targeted"? *Cambridge Review of International Affairs, 29*(3), 912–929.

Pospieszna, P., Skrzypczyńska, J., & Stępień, B. (2020). Hitting two birds with one stone: How Russian countersanctions intertwined political and economic goals. *PS. Political Science & Politics, 53*(2), 243–247.

Quan, K. (2006). *Foreign Ministry spokesman Kong Quan's regular press conference*. Chinese Foreign Ministry. http://www.china-embassy.org/eng/fyrth/t233090.htm

Quinn, C. (2022, June 16). Morning brief: When will sanctions work? *Foreign policy morning brief*.

Rennack, D. E. (2020). *North Korea: Legislative basis for U.S. economic sanctions* (CRS Report No. R41438). U. S. Congressional Research Service. https://crsreports.congress.gov/product/pdf/R/R41438/22

Reuters. (2021, March 12). U.S. engaged in indirect diplomacy with Iran, says white house adviser. *Reuters*. https://www.reuters.com/article/us-iran-nuclear-usa-diplomacy-idUSKBN2B42MO

Reuters. (2022a, March 10). Moscow retaliates against western sanctions with export bans. *Reuters*. https://www.reuters.com/business/russia-suspends-exports-tech-telecoms-medical-auto-agricultural-equipment-until-2022-03-10/

Reuters. (2022b, March 23). Iran's foreign minister says nuclear deal closer 'than ever.' *Reuters*. https://www.reuters.com/world/middle-east/irans-foreign-minister-says-nuclear-deal-closer-than-ever-2022-03-23/

Reuters. (2022c, March 23). U.S. says it is unclear if issues in Iran talks will be resolved. *Reuters*. https://www.reuters.com/world/middle-east/us-says-it-is-unclear-if-issues-iran-talks-will-be-resolved-2022-03-23/

Reuters. (2022d, June 6). Russia sanctions U.S. treasury and energy secretaries, defence and media executives. *Reuters*. https://www.reuters.com/world/russia-sanctions-us-treasury-energy-secretaries-defence-media-bosses-2022-06-06/

Rosenberg, S. (2022, June 14). Russia's economy in for a bumpy ride as sanctions bite. *BBC News.* https://www.bbc.com/news/world-europe-61796067

Rover, J. (2020). "Real" deterrence? Identifying the trump administration's Iran strategy. *Lawfare.* https://www.lawfareblog.com/real-deterrence-identifying-trump-administrations-iran-strategy?fbclid=IwAR1pKbLpzlNbx3F47yUN0jeBkXkmZiDxb_evjVKTFUTx6DMW55Fi0fHgXz0

Ruggiero, A. (2021, December). The Biden team knows its Iran policy is failing. *Foreign Policy.*

Sang-Hun, C. (2020, July 4). In North Korea, coronavirus hurts more than any sanctions could. *The New York Times.* Retrieved January 19, 2021, from https://www.nytimes.com/2020/07/04/world/asia/north-korea-sanctions-coronavirus.html

Scheyder, E., & Soldatkin, V. (2018, February 28). Exxon quits some Russian joint ventures citing sanctions. *Reuters.* Retrieved September 28, 2020, from https://www.reuters.com/article/us-exxon-mobil-russia-rosneft-oil/exxon-quits-some-russian-joint-ventures-citing-sanctions-idUSKCN1GC39B

Sciutto, J., & Bash, D. (2018, March 1). *Nuclear missile threat a 'red line' for Trump on North Korea.* CNN. https://edition.cnn.com/2018/03/01/politics/north-korea-trump-nuclear-missile-threat-red-line/index.html

Statista Research Department. (2022). Total number of restrictive measures imposed on Russia since 2014 and after February 22, 2022 as of June 15, 2022, by selected actor. *In Statista–The Statistics Portal.* Retrieved June 21, 2022, from https://www.statista.com/statistics/1294752/sanctions-imposed-on-russia-by-actor/

Suh, E. (2021, October 1). Biden's North Korea policy. *DGAP online commentary.* https://dgap.org/en/research/publications/bidens-north-korea-policy

Tabuchi, H. (2022, June 13). Russia's oil revenue soars despite sanctions, study finds. *The New York Times.* https://www.nytimes.com/2022/06/13/climate/russia-oil-gas-record-revenue.html

TASS. (2022a, April 27). *Gazprom fully suspends gas supplies to Bulgaria, Poland due to failure to pay in rubles.* TASS. https://tass.com/economy/1443811

TASS. (2022b, May 11). *Russia sanctions 31 energy companies, including ex-subsidiaries of Gazprom in EU.* TASS. https://tass.com/economy/1449571

TASS. (2022c, May 21). *Gazprom confirms stop of Russia's natural gas supplies to Finland.* TASS. https://tass.com/economy/1454141

TASS. (2022d, May 21). *Russian foreign ministry publishes list of 963 US citizens barred from entering Russia.* TASS. https://tass.com/politics/1454179

Timofeev, I. (2022, April 19). Russia-west: Is it possible to lift the sanctions? *Modern Diplomacy.* https://moderndiplomacy.eu/2022/04/19/russia-west-is-it-possible-to-lift-the-sanctions/

The Guardian. (2021, January 9). Kim Jong-UN calls US 'biggest enemy' and says nuclear submarine plans 'complete.' *The Guardian.* https://www.theguardian.com/world/2021/jan/09/kim-jong-un-calls-us-biggest-enemy-and-says-nuclear-submarine-plans-complete

The Wall Street Journal. (2021, January 5). Biden's Iran policy vs reality in Tehran. T*he Wall Street Journal.* https://www.wsj.com/articles/bidens-iran-policy-vs-reality-in-tehran-11609802756

The World Bank. (2020a). *Iran economic monitor: Mitigation and adaptation to sanctions and the pandemic.* http://documents1.worldbank.org/curated/en/229771594197827717/pdf/Iran-Economic-Monitor-Mitigation-and-Adaptation-to-Sanctions-and-the-Pandemic.pdf

The World Bank. (2020b). *World development indicators.*

The White House. (2021, May 21). *U.S.-ROK leaders' joint statement* [Statements and releases]. https://www.whitehouse.gov/briefing-room/statements-releases/2021/05/21/u-s-rok-leaders-joint-statement/

The White House. (2022a, February 9). *Press briefing by press secretary Jen Psaki, February 9, 2022* [Press briefing]. https://www.whitehouse.gov/briefing-room/press-briefings/2022/02/09/press-briefing-by-press-secretary-jen-psaki-february-9-2022/

The White House. (2022b, February 18). P*ress briefing by press secretary Jen Psaki, deputy national security advisor for cyber and emerging technology Anne Neuberger, and deputy national security advisor for international economics and deputy NEC director Daleep Singh,*

References

February 18, 2022 [Press briefing]. https://www.whitehouse.gov/briefing-room/press-briefings/2022/02/18/press-briefing-by-press-secretary-jen-psaki-deputy-national-security-advisor-for-cyber-and-emerging-technology-anne-neuberger-and-deputy-national-security-advisor-for-international-economics-and-dep/

The White House Briefing Room. (2022a, March 8). *Fact Sheet: United States bans imports of Russian oil, liquefied natural gas, and coal* [Fact sheet]. The White House. https://www.whitehouse.gov/briefing-room/statements-releases/2022/03/08/fact-sheet-united-states-bans-imports-of-russian-oil-liquefied-natural-gas-and-coal/

The White House Briefing Room. (2022b, March 11). *Executive order on prohibiting certain imports, exports, and new investment with respect to continued Russian federation aggression.* Presidential Actions [Presidential action]. https://www.whitehouse.gov/briefing-room/presidential-actions/2022/03/11/executive-order-on-prohibiting-certain-imports-exports-and-new-investment-with-respect-to-continued-russian-federation-aggression/

The White House Briefing Room. (2022c, April 6). *Fact sheet: United States, G7 and EU impose severe and immediate costs on Russia* [Fact sheet]. https://www.whitehouse.gov/briefing-room/statements-releases/2022/04/06/fact-sheet-united-states-g7-and-eu-impose-severe-and-immediate-costs-on-russia/

The White House Briefing Room. (2022d, June 2). *Fact Sheet: United States takes further actions to counter sanctions evasion by Russia* [Fact sheet]. https://www.whitehouse.gov/briefing-room/statements-releases/2022/06/02/fact-sheet-united-states-takes-further-actions-to-counter-sanctions-evasion-by-russia/

Tokola, M. (2021). *2021 in review: The Biden administration's North Korea policy* (Vol. December 17). The Peninsula. https://keia.org/the-peninsula/the-biden-administrations-north-korea-policy-in-2021/

Troianovski, A., & Safronova, V. (2022, March 4). Russia takes censorship to new extremes, stifling war coverage. *The New York Times.* https://www.nytimes.com/2022/03/04/world/europe/russia-censorship-media-crackdown.html

Tsebelis, G. (1990). Are sanctions effective? *Journal of Conflict Resolution, 34*(1), 3–28.

UN News. (2022, February 1). *DPR Korea: UN chief condemns missile launch as 'clear violation.'* UN News. https://news.un.org/en/story/2022/02/1111042

UN Panel of Experts. (2013). *Report of the panel of experts established pursuant to resolution 1874 (2009): S/2013/337.* https://undocs.org/S/2013/337

UN Panel of Experts. (2015). *Final report of the panel of experts established pursuant to resolution 1929 (2010): S/2015/401.* https://undocs.org/S/2015/401

UN Panel of Experts. (2019). *Midterm Report of the panel of experts established pursuant to resolution 1874 (2009): S/2019/691.* https://undocs.org/S/2019/691

UN Panel of Experts. (2020). *Report of the panel of experts established pursuant to resolution 1874 (2009): S/2020/151.* https://undocs.org/S/2020/151

UN Security Council. 2016. *Security council strengthens sanctions on democratic Republic of Korea, unanimously adopting resolution 2321 (2016)* [Meeting coverage]. https://www.un.org/press/en/2016/sc12603.doc.htm

U.S. Department of State. (2022a, February 12). *Secretary Antony J. Blinken joint press availability with republic of Korea foreign minister Chung Eui-yong and Japanese foreign minister Hayashi Yoshimasa*. Asia-Pacific center for security studies. https://www.state.gov/secretaryantony-j-blinken-joint-press-availability-with-republic-of-korea-foreign-minister-chung-eui-yong-and-japanese-foreign-minister-hayashiyoshimasa/

U.S. Department of State, Office of the Spokesperson. (2022b, March 3). *Targeting Russian elites and defense enterprises of Russian Federation* [Fact sheet]. U.S. Department of State. https://www.state.gov/targeting-russian-elites-and-defense-enterprises-of-russian-federation/

U.S. Department of State. (2022c, February 24). *U.S. treasury announces unprecedented & expansive sanctions against russia, imposing swift and severe economic costs* [Press Release]. U.S. Department of the treasury. https://home.treasury.gov/news/press-releases/jy0608

U.S. Department of State. (2022d, February 28). T*reasury prohibits transactions with central bank of russia and imposes sanctions on key sources of Russia's wealth*. U.S. Department of the treasury. https://home.treasury.gov/news/press-releases/jy0612

U.S. Department of the Treasury. (2020, May 14). *Guidance to address illicit shipping and sanctions evasion practices* [Advisory]. https://home.treasury.gov/system/files/126/05142020_global_advisory_v1.pdf

U.S. Department of the Treasury. (2021, April 15). *Directive 1 under executive order of April 25, 2021 on blocking property with respect to specified harmful foreign activities of the Government of the Russian Federation*. https://home.treasury.gov/system/files/126/sovereign_debt_prohibition_directive_1.pdf

U.S. Department of the Treasury. (2022a, February 25). *U.S. treasury imposes sanctions on Russian Federation president Vladimir Putin and Minister of Foreign Affairs Sergei Lavrov* [Press release]. https://home.treasury.gov/news/press-releases/jy0610

U.S. Department of the Treasury. (2022b, March 11). *Treasury sanctions kremlin elites, leaders, oligarchs, and family for enabling Putin's war against Ukraine* [Press release]. https://home.treasury.gov/news/press-releases/jy0650

U.S. Department of the Treasury. (2022c, March 24). *U.S. Treasury sanctions Russia's defense-industrial base, the Russian duma and its members, and Sberbank CEO* [Press release]. https://home.treasury.gov/news/press-releases/jy0677

U.S. Department of the Treasury. (2022d, May 22). *Treasury targets oil smuggling network generating hundreds of millions of dollars for Qods force and Hizballah* [Press release]. https://home.treasury.gov/news/press-releases/jy0799

U.S. Department of State, Office of the Spokesperson. (2021). *U.S. sanctions and other measures imposed on Russia in response to Russia's use of chemical weapons* [Fact sheet]. https://www.state.gov/u-s-sanctions-and-other-measures-imposed-on-russia-in-response-to-russias-use-of-chemical-weapons/

Vakulenko, S. (2022, June 14). A big bang? Anticipating the impact of Europe's sanctions on Russian energy. *Eurasian Insight*. Carnegie Endowment for International Peace. https://carnegieendowment.org/eurasiainsight/87318

Vines, A. (2012). The effectiveness of UN and EU sanctions: Lessons for the twenty-first century. *International Affairs, 88*(4), 867–877.

Wallensteen, P., & Grusell, H. (2012). Targeting the right targets? The UN use of individual sanctions. *Global Governance, 18*(2), 207–230.

Weeks, J. L. (2008). Autocratic audience costs: Regime type and signaling resolve. *International Organization, 62*(1), 35–64. http://www.jstor.org/stable/40071874

Wemer, D. (2020, December 10). *The European Magnitsky law—A milestone with a lot of potential*. New Atlanticist. Atlantic Council. https://www.atlanticcouncil.org/blogs/new-atlanticist/the-european-magnitsky-law-a-milestone-with-a-lot-of-potential/

Wertz, D. (2018). The U.S., North Korea, and nuclear diplomacy. *The National Committee on North Korea* https://www.ncnk.org/sites/default/files/issue-briefs/US_DPRK_Relations.pdf.

Whang, T. (2011). Playing to the home crowd? Symbolic use of economic sanctions in the United States. *International Studies Quarterly, 55*(3), 787–801.

Wong, E., Koettl, C., Hurst, W., & Povoledo, E. (2020, March 9). Armored cars, robots and coal: North Korea defies U.S. by evading sanctions. *The New York Times*. https://www.nytimes.com/2020/03/09/world/asia/north-korea-sanctions.html

Yazdani, E., & Hussain, R. (2006). United States' policy towards Iran after the Islamic revolution. *International Studies, 43*(3), 267–289.

GPSR Compliance

The European Union's (EU) General Product Safety Regulation (GPSR) is a set of rules that requires consumer products to be safe and our obligations to ensure this.

If you have any concerns about our products, you can contact us on

ProductSafety@springernature.com

In case Publisher is established outside the EU, the EU authorized representative is:

Springer Nature Customer Service Center GmbH
Europaplatz 3
69115 Heidelberg, Germany

www.ingramcontent.com/pod-product-compliance
Ingram Content Group UK Ltd.
Pitfield, Milton Keynes, MK11 3LW, UK
UKHW021254180426